P...

Stud...

EDITED BY G. M. CARSTAIRS

ALCOHOLISM

Dr Kessel received his medical education at Trinity College, Cambridge, and University College Hospital Medical School in London. His psychiatric training was at the Maudsley Hospital and later he worked at the University of London's Institute of Psychiatry there.

In 1960 he joined the scientific staff of the Medical Research Council, becoming the Assistant Director of the M.R.C. Unit for Research on the Epidemiology of Psychiatric Illness and also a Consultant Psychiatrist at the Royal Infirmary of Edinburgh. He is now Professor of Psychiatry at Manchester University and Director of the Department of Psychiatry of the Manchester Royal Infirmary. His principal researches have been into suicide and self-poisoning acts, psychiatric illness in general practice and psychosomatic illnesses.

Dr Walton is Senior Lecturer in the Department of Psychiatry at Edinburgh University. He is Director of the University Department of Psychiatry at the Western General Hospital, and Consultant Psychiatrist at the Royal Edinburgh Hospital, where he established the Unit for Treatment of Alcoholism. He is a member of the National Council on Alcoholism. Dr Walton is on the Governing Council of the Society for Research into Higher Education, and on the Council of the Association for the Study of Medical Education, and has investigated the effects of different teaching methods in training medical students. He formerly worked at the Maudsley Hospital, and has taught and conducted research at the University of Cape Town and Columbia University in New York. Among the subjects besides alcoholism on which he has published investigations are suicidal behaviour, psychological disturbance in old age, group psychotherapy and professional attitudes of medical practitioners.

Neil Kessel *and* Henry Walton

ALCOHOLISM

PENGUIN BOOKS

Penguin Books Ltd, Harmondsworth, Middlesex, England
Penguin Books Inc., 7110 Ambassador Road, Baltimore, Maryland 21207, U.S.A.
Penguin Books Australia Ltd, Ringwood, Victoria Australia

—

First published 1965
Reprinted with revisions 1967
Reprinted with revisions 1969
Reprinted 1971, 1972

—

—

Made and printed in Great Britain by
Cox & Wyman Ltd, London, Reading and Fakenham
Set in Monotype Garamond

CONTENTS

Throughout this book we have made extensive use of reports of the experiences of patients who have been under our care, and we wish here to acknowledge our debt to them.

EDITORIAL FOREWORD

ANIMALS, no less than man, inherit powerful instinctive drives to preserve their life and liberty; but the pursuit of happiness is a peculiarly human characteristic – as old, no doubt, as the dawn of consciousness and with it the heightened awareness of our own states of mind – and so has been the search for drugs to facilitate this pursuit.

One of the earliest steps in the history of man was the cultivation of cereals; but already in very ancient archaeological sites there is evidence that these grains were used not only as food, but also in the preparation of a fermented brew, the precursor of beer.

Nearly every society appears to have discovered substances which powerfully influence the mind, lightening fatigue and the burden of care, promoting fellow-feeling and at least a temporary sense of well-being. All over the world, a variety of these mood-elevating substances, such as coffee, tea, cocoa, hashish, peyotl and opium, have been in use for centuries before the tranquillizers were invented, and these are still the preferred tranquillizer in certain areas. In our own society, however, and throughout the Western world, the traditional euphoriant has always been alcohol, in one of its many preparations.

Many of these euphoriants are relatively harmless; strong coffee in excess can damage the heart, but tea and cocoa are innocuous, and although both peyotl and hashish can be profoundly intoxicating, they seem to confer no lasting ill effects. This cannot, of course, be said for opium or its derivatives, nor of cocaine; and alcohol seems to occupy an intermediate position. Used in moderation, its undoubted social usefulness is not accompanied by any serious ill effects; but the trouble is, of course, that some people find it extremely difficult to take alcohol only in moderation, and instead become dependent upon it, thus exposing themselves to serious physical and mental consequences.

Our society has, it seems, made a hazardous choice in adopting alcohol as its customary form of solace against 'the thousand natural shocks that flesh is heir to'; and the ambiguity which characterizes our attitudes towards alcohol reflects our awareness that it is a boon to many, and a scourge to some members of our society.

This book is about alcoholism, that is, about alcohol in its harmful aspect. It is written by two experienced psychiatrists who not only are well versed in scientific research on alcoholism to which each of them has made valuable contributions but also have the gift of translating research findings into lucid and arresting prose. They have set themselves the task of answering most, if not all, of the fundamental questions which present themselves to any thoughtful person who encounters the tragedy of alcoholism in his work, among his friends, or in a member of his family.

Drinking takes on a completely new connotation when one is thus brought face to face with its tragic consequences: this prompts one to think again about the physical and mental effects of alcohol, in moderate as well as in excessive doses. The serious havoc which drink can wreak with the happiness of alcoholics and their families quickens one's interest in finding out why it is that a substance which gladdens the lives of so many should darken the lives of some.

The account which Professor Kessel and Dr Walton give of the causes and the social repercussions of excessive drinking is informed by their own extensive experience of treating these unfortunate individuals. As they show, with numerous recent examples, this is an area of medico-psychiatric care in which scientific knowledge has to be allied with a sustained concern for the unhappy victims of alcoholism in their laborious efforts to regain their self-control and self-respect.

The study ends, appropriately, with a consideration of alcoholism as a public-health problem. There have been periods in our social history (the latest occurring in the aftermath of the Industrial Revolution) when alcoholism was especially associated with poverty and squalor. Deliberate social policies have intervened to change this situation by controlling the availability of alcohol, limiting the age of its purchasers, and greatly increasing the price of spirits.

Today, the picture is a different one. Alcoholism continues to take its toll not only in the unhappiness of individual patients and their families, but also indirectly in other ways – for example, by its significant contribution to the causes of death on the roads – but now it has become one of the gravest manifestations of social pathology even among the better-off members of our affluent societies. In quite recent years it has been noticeable that teenagers, as a result of their increased spending money, are also becoming increasingly involved in excessive drinking, and some are presenting the clinical picture of severe alcoholism while still in their twenties. There are clearly challenges here: there is the need, which is only belatedly being recognized, for effective treatment for the victims of alcoholism, but there is also an urgent need for greater understanding on the part of the general public about the nature of this problem, and about how it can best be tackled. This book will, I believe, contribute towards that wider understanding.

G. M. Carstairs

PREFACE

THE difference between having a drink and becoming drunk depends upon the quantity of alcohol taken. The amount needed to intoxicate will vary from person to person and from time to time, but anyone who drinks enough will get drunk. Between the drinker and the alcoholic there is another kind of difference. It cannot be measured in amount of alcohol nor even be shortly defined. It depends upon intangibles, upon personality and upon opportunity, upon circumstance and often upon chance. Yet the steps from social to excessive drinking can be demarcated and it is the extent of his passage along this road that defines the alcoholic. Until he embarked upon it he was not obviously different from his fellows, although to the expert observer there might have been indications that he was predisposed.

We live in a society where it is customary to drink. It is the abstainer who strikes us as the more abnormal. With alcohol we offer hospitality and display our sociability. Though we frown on drunkards we are suspicious of teetotallers. Over a glass we enjoy old friends and make new ones, proclaim our loyalties, discuss affairs, negotiate and seal bargains. Repeated minimal intoxication is expected of our leading figures, soldiers, statesmen, businessmen, dons. We know that this sort of drinking, open and well moderated, is, for the most part, harmless and seems to conduce to good relationships.

In most cultures social drinking is approved for the release which alcohol permits to an individual. At solemn ceremonies marking epochal events, birth, marriage and death, in religious ritual, in national celebration, in sporting victory and to mark the modest achievements of everyday life, alcohol has an honoured and accustomed place. It reduces tension. Its merit is to help people join together to form groups.

Strangers relax and mingle if alcohol is provided. A man provides drinks when for reasons of hospitality or business he wants to create an atmosphere of warmth in a gathering of people who do not know each other well. Nor does he have to hide his intention, for his guests welcome his social engineering. Though they may have few interests in common, these they will discover. Drinks will make them socialize. Less apprehensive of their own failings, they will become less inclined to judge others critically. Oiling the social wheels is at the centre of society's approbation of regulated drinking.

The individual, for his part, has a double impetus to drink. He is complying with the social pattern and the effects of drinking are pleasurable. People do not drink only to attain particular mental or physical sensations. They are conforming to situations in which drinking is proper.

We are tolerant of the man who has a drink, or even a drink too many. The alcoholic also once drank moderately like this. What made him cross the line into alcoholism? Were the causes within him, inexorably at work, or did they lie in his environment and in his life circumstances? Physical, social and psychological factors have all to be considered. What is the course on which he is now set? Where does the road lead and is there a way back? This book deals with these questions.

The magnitude and importance of the illness of alcoholism are insufficiently appreciated. It is a grave disorder, often fatal. Its impact falls not only on the alcoholic but on a wide circle of family and friends. Its social reverberations affect accident and crime rates, absenteeism and unemployment. It is one of the most prominent causes of mental hospital admissions. Yet in many quarters, both medical and lay, this major threat to public health and welfare is not given serious consideration.

We shall deal in this book first with the physical and the psychological effects of alcoholism. Then social and psycho-

logical factors conducing to alcoholism will be discussed and
the causes of alcoholism will be reviewed. Subsequent chap-
ters will describe types of alcoholics and the progressive stages
of the disease. Finally we set out some principles of treatment
and prevention.

Chapter 1

WHAT IS AN ALCOHOLIC?

THREE factors conspire to make alcoholism a difficult subject to grasp and to study. Because many of the antics of the inebriated are good for a laugh people often joke about alcoholics. What is, in fact, a considerable medical and social problem is thus eased out of serious consideration with a smile. Secondly, moral overtones colour our opinions, making it hard to amass information and arrive at proper judgements. Consequently an objective assessment of the alcoholic is difficult. A girl who gets drunk at a party, a man who drives a car when intoxicated, someone who spends so much on drink that his family's well-being is affected – with what words do we appraise them? Censure, blame, condemnation, disgust? Or do we despise, ostracize, punish? Almost certainly we do not sympathize, feel responsible or try to understand. However, to study the problem of alcoholism scientifically it is necessary to be free of condemnatory attitudes. Moreover, such an approach is essential if anyone, doctor or friend, is to be accepted by an alcoholic as competent to understand and help him.

Lastly, the problem of alcoholism is made more difficult by lack of technical terms which are generally understood. What is an alcoholic? Without being adequately defined the term is too readily applied to embrace everybody who drinks abnormally. Not all these are alcoholics. Furthermore, there are many different types of alcoholics and many varied patterns of alcoholism. Some define the alcoholic from the vantage point of the sufferer; they name as an alcoholic the person who recognizes that he has to stop drinking but cannot do so. Others have focused on the observable consequences of uncontrolled drinking; they define an alcoholic as a person whose drinking has caused increasing problems in his health, his domestic or social life or with his work. Others emphasize the quantity of alcohol consumed and the pattern of the drinking habits; only the man who regularly drinks till he is helpless is an alcoholic from their point of view.

A frame of reference is necessary if the subject is not to remain nebulous. While the social aspects of alcoholism are very important we prefer to think of alcoholism as a medical condition and shall use the following terminology.

Some people are *teetotallers*.

Most people drink moderately. They may from time to time get drunk. These are *social drinkers*.

Some people drink excessively, though not necessarily in their own eyes; their excess may show either by the frequency with which they become intoxicated or by the social, economic, or medical consequences of their continued intake of alcohol. These are *excessive drinkers*. Those excessive drinkers whose drinking gives rise to personal and social difficulties would do well not to equivocate but to recognize that alcohol lies at the root of their problem. Many excessive drinkers who have growing difficulties arising from their use of alcohol may be in serious need of medical care and can respond to appropriate treatment. However, it is important to grasp that not all excessive drinkers are alcoholics, though probably the great majority of them proceed to this next stage.

Alcoholics are people with a disease that can be defined in medical terms and requires a proper régime of treatment. Alcoholics are addicted to alcohol. *Alcohol addicts* are unable spontaneously to give up drinking. Though they may go without a drink for a few days, or sometimes for even longer periods inevitably they revert. The greater the need to stop drinking the more difficult do they find it to do so. Besides this characteristic of the alcohol addict,[1] that he cannot go for long without alcohol, he generally suffers from withdrawal symptoms – short-lived (though often serious) physical or mental ill-effects which supervene when drinking is temporarily halted for a few days or even hours.

Most alcoholics proceed to a stage where their brains or their bodies have been so harmed by alcohol that the effects persist even when they are not drinking. This stage may be reached by some excessive drinkers who had not manifested addiction. It is called *chronic alcoholism*. The term should only be applied when the body has been physically damaged by alcohol.

To classify a particular drinker may not be easy, yet it is essential if he is to be helped. We cannot properly proceed until we know whether he is a social drinker, an excessive drinker, an excessive drinker with problems, an alcoholic (i.e. an alcohol addict), or has reached the further stage of chronic alcoholism.

Addiction to alcohol is different from addiction to most dangerous drugs, such as opium, heroin, and cocaine. In the first place, addiction to alcohol is far more accepted by society because drinking is to a large extent socially condoned. Secondly, drug addicts may work up to a dose far exceeding what would be fatal to an ordinary person; alcohol addicts on the other hand do not require to go on increasing their intake in the same way. Although the habituated alcoholic is not as affected by alcohol as the novice drinker, nevertheless he does not need to drink greatly increased quantities to continue to get the desired effect. When the drug addict stops he experiences a craving; physiological changes set up a subjective need for more of the drug. He also develops withdrawal symptoms which are promptly alleviated by another single dose. The alcoholic may be able to abstain for quite long periods without craving, particularly if he is in a hospital or other institution.

1. For reasons given on pages 17 and 18, some prefer the term 'dependent'.

If he does experience withdrawal effects they are generally not abolished by a single further drink. The term addict, however, is appropriate to alcoholics in one very important sense. All addicts are *dependent* upon the substances they take. They may not, in the case of alcohol, require it constantly, nor does the need necessarily betoken physical dependence. It may be a psychological dependence, so that the alcoholic may rely on alcohol, either continuously or from time to time, to free him from unbearable tensions. With its aid he can face his problems, his family and himself. He is dependent upon alcohol to function efficiently as a social being. It is the irony of this which makes alcoholism into a problem, for the very stuff on which he relies in order to function has the inexorable physiological effect of impairing function.

To resolve this situation, to help the alcoholic to be able to conduct his life without alcohol, is called 'treatment'. So we can now understand the whole of the World Health Organization definition[1] of the alcoholic:

Alcoholics are those excessive drinkers whose dependence on alcohol has attained such a degree that they show a noticeable mental disturbance or an interference with their mental and bodily health, their interpersonal relations and their smooth social and economic functioning; or who show the prodromal signs of such developments.

They therefore require treatment.

'Treatment' suggests something which only doctors can give. But the help which alcoholics require has to be given by those associated with them, family, friends and employers as well as social agencies and physicians. Directly or indirectly alcoholism is everyone's concern.

It is a growing problem. The World Health Organization[2] has

1. World Health Organization. Expert Committee on Mental Health (1952). *Alcohol Subcommittee Second Report.* W.H.O. Technical Report Series, No. 48.

2. Expert Committee on Mental Health (1951). *Report on the First Session of the Alcoholism Subcommittee.* W.H.O. Technical Report No. 42, Annex 2.

estimated that there are 350,000 alcoholics in Britain, a quarter
of whom show physical and mental deterioration. The size of
this figure clearly argues the magnitude of the problem, though
in our opinion estimates like this are not reliable. It is difficult
to see how an accurate count can be obtained. Alcoholism is not
a notifiable disease nor is it definable in unambiguous, operational terms so that everyone can readily agree whether or not
someone is an alcoholic. Moreover, many alcoholics do not
come to any agency interested in counting them. General practitioners, for instance, know of only about a ninth of the alcoholics among their registered patients.[1] In general hospitals,
many alcoholics are treated for physical illnesses without their
alcoholism being diagnosed or recorded. Data are, however,
available about admissions to psychiatric hospitals. In England
and Wales in 1959, 26 men and 6 women per million of the
population, respectively, were admitted *for the first time* with a
diagnosis of alcoholism or alcoholic psychoses.[2] The corresponding rates for Scotland (1961) were 175 men and 30
women.[3] (Alcoholism here refers to Code 322 of the International Statistical Classification of Diseases and Causes of
Death.) These Scottish rates are seven times as high for men,
five times for women.

Of course, only a small proportion of alcoholics are ever
admitted to a psychiatric hospital. Most never get there. Some
die without ever receiving psychiatric treatment. Alcoholism
is a killing disease: cirrhosis of the liver, malnutrition, road
accidents and suicide all take a heavy toll. Although there are
no reliable figures for deaths in which excessive drinking plays
a part, physicians who see a lot of the problem know that the

1. Parr, D. (1957). 'Alcoholism in general practice'. *British Journal of Addiction, 54*, 25.

2. Registrar General (1962). *Statistical Review of England and Wales for the year 1959. Supplement on Mental Health.* London: H.M.S.O.

3. General Board of Control for Scotland (1957–62). *Annual Reports for the years 1956 to 1961.* Edinburgh: H.M.S.O.

established alcoholic who is not successfully treated has a
greatly reduced expectation of life. This is reflected in the
official statistics of the Registrar General showing the grossly
increased mortality of people in high risk occupations.
Publicans, for instance, have a death rate from cirrhosis of the
liver nine times as high as for all men of comparable age.[1]

None of these sources satisfactorily answer the question of
how many alcoholics there are? The World Health Organization statistics are based on a formula which uses the figures for
deaths registered as due to cirrhosis of the liver. This implies
that one can know both the percentage of such deaths that are
due to alcohol and the percentage of alcoholics who develop
this liver disease. But we do not. The only way in which we
could really find out the size of the alcoholic population would
be by going into the community and counting them. Such a
survey would present considerable difficulties and has never been
done in Britain. A recent household study[2] in a mixed racial
residential area of New York City (Washington Heights)
revealed three men and one woman per 100 population aged
20 or over who had drinking problems. Most of these disclosed
the fact themselves to the interviewers. An approach to a solution would be to ask key people in the community such as
general practitioners, clergymen and police to list the alcoholics
they know. But the more 'key people' you ask the more
alcoholics you will find. The eventual estimate arrived at will
reflect the extent of the search and must always be an approxi-
mation. Such an approach was used in Cambridgeshire,[3] and
showed that 6·2 of every thousand adult men (women, 1·4)
were alcoholic.

1. Registrar General (1957). *Decennial Supplement, England and Wales,
1951. Occupational Mortality, Part 2, Vol. 2.* London: H.M.S.O.

2. Bailey, M. B., Haberman, P. W. and Alksne, H. (1965). 'The Epidemiology of Alcoholism in an Urban Residential Area'. *Quarterly Journal
of Studies on Alcohol, 26,* 19.

3. Moss, M. C. and Beresford Davies, E. (1968). 'A Survey of Alcoholism
in an English County'. Privately printed, Geigy (U.K.) Ltd.

Do we need to know the exact prevalence? The only practical reason for wanting it is to determine the need for services and we are already sure that whether there are 500,000 or 50,000 alcoholics in Britain, present services, both social and medical, fall far short of requirements.

So far we have looked at the size of the problem primarily from a medical standpoint. The fact that alcoholism is a disease should be more generally appreciated in Britain both by the public and by doctors. In 1935 the American Medical Association passed a resolution that: 'Alcoholics are valid patients.' This is the counterpart of W.H.O.'s: 'They therefore deserve treatment.' In Britain many doctors and others responsible for organizing medical services are loath to accept this.

Alcoholism also poses social problems both for the community and for the individual alcoholic and his family. In most cities there are to be found depressed areas where alcoholics congregate, limbos where they eke out poverty-stricken, degenerate, sometimes psychotic existences. Alcoholism leads to absenteeism and unemployment, debt, crime, social decline and sometimes child neglect. The average family in Britain spends 13s. 6d. a week on drink, about four per cent of its weekly expenditure, but in an alcoholic's household the proportion can easily become ten times as much.

There are other social ills which, if they cannot directly be laid at the door of alcoholism, are certainly related to it. There is highly suggestive evidence that alcoholics swell the numbers of arrests for drunkenness and are responsible for many road accidents due to drinking. We discuss this in Chapter 13.

Recently there has been a steep rise in convictions for the offence of drunkenness and it is especially worrying that this increase has been noteworthy even for people under the age of 21. In the Metropolitan Police District of London alone, in 1963 there were 35,485 convictions for drunkenness and 1,587 of these were of youths under 21. Those concerned to sell drink have long been aiming to attract women into the pub, thus securing the custom of their male friends. More recently they have been beaming their advertisements particularly at teen-agers.[1] The increase in drinking by youngsters is now being reflected clinically by an increase in the number of established alcoholics still in their twenties. Many of these will die in their thirties.

Whether an alcoholic is viewed as a medical or as a social problem will profoundly affect the future course of his disorder. Where the alcoholic is dealt with by the courts he is likely to spend time in jail in an atmosphere that is both custodial and punitive, not directed at his rehabilitation. Where medical treatment is available and doctors are prepared to accept responsibility for the management of his condition, the institution to which the alcoholic is admitted is more likely to be a hospital. The measures adopted then will be therapeutic, designed to foster his self-respect and sustain his resolve to overcome his disability. Today in Britain each method is applied and the disposal generally depends not upon the individual's needs but on the relatively trivial circumstance that brings him to the notice of one or other service. Anyone responsible for dealing with an alcoholic ought to obtain all the information he can, medical and social, and reflect seriously in every case whether the allocation decided upon fits the individual requirements.

1. Advertising Inquiry Council (1961). *Report on Drink Advertising.* London.

Chapter 2

THE NATURE OF ALCOHOL AND ITS INTOXICATING EFFECTS

THE chemist recognizes many different alcohols. The one we drink is called *ethyl alcohol*. Carbon, hydrogen and oxygen are its only chemical elements. They exist in simple combination to form a colourless liquid. Two linked atoms of carbon have five hydrogen atoms attached to form the ethyl radical. A hydroxyl (or alcohol) group completes the chemical molecule. In the diagram, C, H and O stand for single atoms of carbon, hydrogen and oxygen; —OH denotes the hydroxyl group.

$$
\begin{array}{ccc}
\text{H} & \text{H} & \\
| & | & \\
\text{H} - \text{C} - \text{C} &\!\!\!\!\!\!\!\!\! - \!\!\!\!\!\!\!\!\! & \text{OH} \\
| & | & \\
\text{H} & \text{H} &
\end{array}
$$

ethyl   alcohol

Other alcohols can be made by adding or subtracting carbon and hydrogen atoms, but only the ethyl variety has the conventional effects of alcohol as we know them and only ethyl alcohol is safe to consume. Alcohol can be prepared easily from many plants and has been known to man from earliest times all over the world.

Although the chemist can make it from its basic constituents the alcohol we drink comes from fermentation by yeast of sugars that occur naturally in plants. The drinks produced by such fermentation, beer from barley, wine from grapes and cider from apples, are relatively weak in alcohol. Beer contains between $2\frac{1}{2}$ and $4\frac{1}{2}$ per cent alcohol by volume. Strong beers have as much as 8 per cent; ciders are roughly of comparable strength. Most wines contain between 10 per cent and 12 per cent of alcohol. The alcohol concentration may be increased subsequently by distillation, a process which produces spirits.

The strength of spirits is much greater. In Britain they generally contain between 30 per cent and 40 per cent of alcohol, more in the United States. Forty per cent is the usual strength in this country for gin and whisky (though some malt whiskies are stronger). Rum, brandy and vodka are of similar but more variable strength. The strength of liqueurs varies widely. The strength of spirits is generally recorded as so many 'degrees proof'. This harks back to an old measure of the concentration of alcohol devised by the early distillers. Gunpowder mixed with water will not ignite but mixed with alcohol it will. If mixtures of alcohol and water are tried it is found that a combination of half alcohol, half water will allow the gunpowder to ignite but weaker concentrations of alcohol will not. The strength of the spirit used to be *proved* in this way. Proof spirit contains approximately 57 per cent of alcohol by volume; 70 degrees proof means that the alcohol content is about 40 per cent.

Some drinks are mixtures of ferments and distillates. Sherry, for instance, is a fortified wine, brandy being added to bring the alcohol strength up to 20 per cent.

No matter what beverage is drunk the alcoholic effect depends on the amount of alcohol consumed and not on the colouring, flavouring or any other constituents, though there is currently some interest in the independent effects of these other components of alcoholic beverages, known as congeners.

Alcohol exerts, according to its strength, an effect on the lining of the mouth, the oesophagus, the stomach and the upper part of the intestines. In the mouth this is experienced as a burning sensation, pleasant or slightly painful. The expression 'that hits the spot!' well describes the stinging and the satisfying effects of a glass of spirits quickly drunk. From the stomach and intestines the alcohol is absorbed into the blood stream and passes rapidly into all the tissues and fluids of the body. Gradually it is destroyed by oxidation, principally in the liver, and it is eventually broken down into carbon dioxide and water. A small quantity, perhaps 2 per cent, escapes this process and is excreted in the urine and in the breath. The amount of alcohol breathed out is very small indeed, but it is sufficient to indicate the concentration of alcohol in the body. The smell on a drinker's breath is imparted chiefly by other volatile constituents of drinks and is no index of the extent of intoxication. The rate at which alcohol is oxidized is independent of the concentration in the body; as the maximum rate is quickly reached it follows that it will take much longer for someone who has drunk very heavily to return to normal than it does for a moderate drinker. Four ounces of whisky or four pints of beer might take four or five hours to be oxidized and if the amount drunk is doubled it would take twice as long. For this reason people who drink slowly but continuously, though they may appear less incapable, take as long to recover from drinking as those who have absorbed a similar quantity rapidly.

The principal effects of alcohol are upon the nervous system but changes also occur elsewhere in the body. The heart rate may rise a little and there is an increased flow in the blood vessels resulting in flushing and a warm sensation in the skin. The rate of urine production rises, chiefly as a consequence of the amount of fluid that is drunk but also because alcohol influences the pituitary gland which controls the rate of urine formation.

Alcohol is a food. As a provider of calories it must, in Britain, be one of the most expensive, and certainly the most extensively taxed. It is a carbohydrate and because of its rapid absorption from the stomach it is a quick source of energy. However, this energy cannot be used efficiently because of the incoordinating and intoxicating effects of alcohol. Only the self-deceiving can believe they are doing something dietetically useful by drinking, except for stimulating the appetite.

Alcohol is supposed to be an aphrodisiac and to promote sexual function. It may stimulate desire, and the shy man or the cautious may, under its influence, be able to have intercourse because his inhibitions, his fears or his scruples have been lessened. However, this is a psychological effect. Upon potency alcohol exerts a dampening action.

The effect of alcohol upon the nervous system is to reduce its activities. All its functions are depressed. How is it, therefore, that alcohol has come to be widely thought of as a stimulant? Unless we can resolve this paradox we shall never understand the use of alcohol by man.

Let us marshal the evidence for stating so categorically that it depresses activity in the nervous system. On the physical side it numbs like an anaesthetic so that a man may fall when drunk and not appreciate that he has hurt himself; it may send him to sleep; it may even make him unconscious. It alters the rhythm of brain waves recorded electrically from the head. Even in small amounts it affects speech and balance and impairs judgement. After a few drinks our ability to react promptly to a changing situation or an emergency is reduced, so that we ought not to drive a car. In ordinary social intercourse, at a party for instance, we can no longer so finely or so quickly assess what it is proper for us to say or to keep silent about. Here lies the explanation of the paradox. The first thing to be depressed is the power of restraint. The inhibition of our actions or our wishes which we all of us adopt in order to get on with our fellows is the product of the highest mental processes and it is these that are impaired first. When the curb we normally place on our instinctual urges goes, unguarded behaviour comes to the fore and these released impulses are forcefully expressed, giving the impression of stimulation. The solitary become gregarious, shy men loquacious and the fearful foolhardy. Self-critical men can treat themselves kindly, sexually inhibited men dare to be amorous. As our individual characteristics drop away from us attributes common to us all prevail. At first the increased press of talk and activity sets up smiles, gaiety, even boisterousness. Generally we retain enough self-control to keep these within bounds. Most social drinking never proceeds farther than this and the atmosphere produced is indeed stimulating. It is also infectious. In Sweden, for instance, where it is usual for one member of a party not to drink because he will be driving home, the communal laughter, affection and good spirits rub off on to him as well so that he shares in the general feeling of well-being.

But sometimes the drinking facilitates a group mood of dejection or of anger, and people have had their passions so inflamed by alcohol that they carried out cruel, senseless, irrevocable actions from which, if the highest mental processes were functioning intact, each individual would recoil with disgust. This, of course, is the extreme, but the morning-after reaction sometimes contains a sense of amazement and shame that one could have done the things one did so carelessly the night before.

These changes, which the physician and the physiologist call depression of the nervous system, begin with the first drink. There is not a level below which one can drink without any noticeable change but above which one is affected. Fine tests of discrimination, of memory, of driving skills all show that the impairment begins with the beginning of drinking and advances steadily with the continuation of drinking. We know too that a vicious circle is set up. The more we drink, the more our faculties and our judgement are lost, and consequently the less we appreciate this falling off of our skills. It is this which allows clearly incapable men to believe they are fit to drive. In a recent experiment[1] bus drivers, after drinking different amounts, were asked to judge whether they could get their buses between two movable posts. As they drank more and more they became less

1. Cohen, J., Dearnaley, E. J. and Hansel, C. E. M. (1958). 'The risk taken in driving under the influence of alcohol'. *British Medical Journal*, 1, 1438.

accurate in deciding, but more certain that they were right. This is one reason why it is impossible to state an amount to drink or a blood concentration of alcohol below which it is all right to drive. For legal purposes an arbitrary level may have to be fixed but the truth is that *some* impairment occurs with any drinking, one small whisky, half a pint of beer. The drinker is in the worst possible position to make the decision whether he is safe to drive or not.

During a single episode of drinking a certain level of alcohol concentration in the blood will be achieved, and then as further drinking takes place it will be exceeded. Later on, as the drinker sobers up, the blood concentration will again pass the former level as it falls. But if we make psychological observations at two points in time when blood concentration is the same, one when it is rising and one when it is falling, we cannot fail to observe that he performs better on the later occasion.

Neither the amount that is drunk nor the blood alcohol level, therefore, can be absolute guides to a person's capabilities.

Another reason why it is dangerous to lay down safe amounts to drink is that increased tolerance occurs in drinkers. This phenomenon explains why not all people who drink the same amount become equally intoxicated. Different people are differently affected by the same intake of alcohol. Some have more tolerance than others; that is to say, their efficiency is less impaired. An individual develops increased tolerance during the course of his drinking career; at the outset he will be much more affected, say, by six whiskies than he will be later on. Still later, especially if he falls sick or is undernourished, his tolerance may again decline. This accounts for the distressing experience of many advanced alcoholics that suddenly they become much more disorganized by an amount of drink which previously they could handle without difficulty.

During the process of acquiring tolerance the cells of the body become seasoned to alcohol so that a given concentration affects them less than it used to. No one knows how tolerance develops. It has nothing to do with the rate of absorption, metabolism or excretion of alcohol. All we can say is that the cells of the body, in particular of the brain, get used to functioning in the presence of higher concentrations of alcohol than they could tolerate before.

Chapter 3

THE HARMFUL EFFECTS OF ALCOHOL ON THE BRAIN AND THE BODY

You cannot look at a stranger and say with confidence from his appearance that he is an alcoholic. It is easy to tell that a man is drunk but not that he is an habitual drinker. Yet continued excessive drinking does produce bodily changes and these in turn result in illnesses both physical and mental.

From the somatic standpoint the most serious consequence of alcoholism is malnutrition. This arises in two ways. The chronic alcoholic does not eat enough and what he eats does not nourish him as well as it should. He does not eat enough partly because his earnings may be small but chiefly because he redistributes his spending so as to buy more and more drink and consequently less and less food. Drinking becomes a more pressing necessity than eating. Also, he is frequently forced to fend for himself because his wife and relations have left him. His knowledge about cooking and the facilities for it are both probably inadequate so he will fall back on the comparatively expensive practice of buying prepared foods. His diet will be excessively starchy and considerably deficient in protein. If he takes his food in pubs so as to be able to drink at the same time he is likely to subsist chiefly on rolls, potato crisps, and occasional sausages. The high price of food in public houses constitutes a further economic setback. He will get enough in sheer calories, however, because of the alcohol. Besides the protein lack, such a diet is deficient in vitamins, particularly in vitamin B.

These considerations apply more to the poor than to the rich alcoholic. But even he is likely to suffer from missed meals and from self-induced restrictions of diet because his appetite has gone. He prefers to forgo solid for liquid refreshment.

The lack of appetite (*anorexia*) is often accompanied by morning nausea which leads to giving up breakfast; during the day the constant supply of alcoholic calories between meals reduces feelings of hunger, and the effect of an inflamed stomach (*gastritis*) or of a diseased liver (*cirrhosis*) is to produce further anorexia. These factors, independently or in concert, may result in an even more serious nutritional deficiency for, when they operate, food may not be properly absorbed from the intestines or metabolized for the body's use. Ultimately a vicious circle is set up. Malnutrition itself contributes to cirrhosis of the liver, resulting in further malnutrition. Once the alcoholic reaches a certain stage of physical change his further decline is generally rapid.

Chronic alcoholism is the commonest cause of liver disease. We cannot be sure whether the alcohol exerts a direct toxic effect on the liver cells or whether the poor absorption of food from the intestine and the poor diet together produce an insufficiency of some substances essential to the liver's good repair. The important thing is that chronic alcoholics frequently suffer from liver disease which may in its early stages be mild and reversible but which, if unchecked, can progress to the severe form which is called cirrhosis (because of the scarring and hardening which the liver undergoes). The chief clinical features are a feeling of illness (liverishness is the name given to its mild form), flatulence, anorexia and sallowness of the skin. About a third of all cases develop jaundice. Dropsy and vomiting of blood may both occur late in the disease, which kills about half of those who suffer from it.

Before he develops cirrhosis the alcoholic is likely to suffer fairly severely from gastritis. Indeed some purely social drinkers are affected by this condition to such an extent that the pain and flatulence actually stop them from drinking any further on particular occasions. The inflammation of the stomach from which the condition gets its name is caused directly by the irritant property of strong drinks; spirits cause it more than beer or wine. The stomach's blood-vessels become dilated so that the whole lining is suffused with blood and covered in mucus. In addition, the stomach ceases to contract normally but distends, giving rise to discomfort and flatulence. Gastritis is the simplest of all the alcoholic conditions to cure. It goes away quickly once drinking stops.

The remaining physical illnesses brought about by chronic alcoholism are borne by the nervous system. An important cause is malnutrition resulting in a deficiency of one or more of the B vitamins. This is responsible for a common condition, peripheral neuritis. The nerve fibres bear the brunt of this condition and the longer nerves, those which stretch all the way from the spinal column to the ends of the limbs are the most involved because their need for vitamins is greatest. Hence the neuritis is 'peripheral'. It mainly affects the toes and the feet, the fingers and the hands, beginning with a sensation of tingling, pins and needles, and progressing to numbness. Because the nerves to the skin are affected the sufferer cannot finely assess what he is touching and may not know that there is anything in his hand if he does not look. He cannot appreciate ups and downs in the surface he walks upon and feels that he is treading all the time on cotton-wool. In a late stage the nerves to the joints become damaged so that the patient may no longer know the positions that his feet or hands are in. Consequently he keeps on falling. The sensory nerves are affected earlier than those responsible for muscular movement, but as the condition progresses these also suffer and weakness develops, first in the extremities and later spreading towards the trunk. Peripheral neuritis requires treatment in bed. Vitamin B therapy is necessary and it may take many months before recovery is complete.

These physical ravages of alcoholism occur, for obvious reasons, late in its course. If treatment is not commenced and vigorously carried out, the patient (for by this time a patient he certainly is) is likely to pursue a progressive downhill course towards invalidism and death. Fortunately he can no longer evade medical attention and, provided that his physician does not enter into a covert conspiracy with him to gloss over the true nature of his condition, he may be persuaded into accepting treatment to make him give up drinking.

So far we have discussed the damage done to the body by excessive drinking. We must now turn to abnormal mental states which arise from the effects on the brain of prolonged excessive intake. Mental symptoms of chronic alcoholism may be caused in three ways; they may occur as withdrawal symptoms or from vitamin deficiency or from destruction of brain cells.

Withdrawal symptoms are brought about by stopping drinking or by a sudden drastic reduction in the amount taken. In consequence there is a rapid drop in the concentration of alcohol in the blood. Heavy drinkers of some years' duration, who maintain a very high alcohol intake continuously for some days or weeks before stopping, are sensitive to this reduction in concentration and develop symptoms. The same symptoms which follow alcohol withdrawal can also be produced by the sudden cutting off of barbiturate sleeping tablets by anyone who has been heavily overdosed for some time. Because of this similarity in withdrawal symptoms, alcohol and barbiturates are classified in the same group of addictive agents.

Symptoms occur anything from a few hours to a few days after stopping drinking. Milder symptoms begin earlier; delirium tremens, the most severe, begins late. The earliest and commonest withdrawal state is *acute tremulousness*. This is what physicians call it but alcoholics know it as 'the shakes'. It follows so soon upon reduction in heavy drinking that it may in fact come on before drinking has completely stopped. Usually, however, it takes a few hours to develop and many alcoholics are consequently affected by it each morning. 'When I wake up I have to take a drink to steady myself' is a common complaint. In this state the alcoholic is agitated, jumpy and easily startled. The principal feature is gross shaking of the hands, made worse if he tries to do anything with them. Sometimes he complains of feeling shaky inside. There is anxiety, physical restlessness and a feeling of weakness. Agitation and tremor can reach such a degree that he may not be able to sit still, to dress himself or to pour out a drink without spilling it. Usually the condition disappears fairly rapidly as more drink is taken but without alcohol it may persist for as long as a week or more. More severe forms of alcoholic tremulousness occur in spree drinkers after many days of unrelieved drinking; the continuous drinker is usually subject to milder forms. A quarter of those who suffer moderate or severe attacks have accompanying hallucinations. These are usually short-lived and may only be admitted to after they have ceased to be experienced. Then the alcoholic says that he had a vivid nightmare which was difficult to disentangle from reality. The hallucinations may be visual or auditory. Things around him may appear distorted in shape; shadows seem to be real and to move. Shouting or snatches of music may be heard and he may also misinterpret innocent remarks of bystanders whether they are addressed to him or not. If the alcoholic is examined at this time, especially if he is in the unfamiliar surroundings of a hospital or police station, he may have a little difficulty in orientation, in conveying where he is and what time it is.

Delirium tremens is one of the most dramatic conditions in the whole calendar of medicine. To the observer there is a rapidly changing picture of bewildering, disordered mental activity. It is difficult for him to realize that for the sufferer every conscious moment is one of extreme fear. Fear, agitation and great distractibility are the dominant features, although disorientation and hallucination are the most vivid. Delirium tremens – DTs – generally begins two to five days after stopping very heavy drinking. It may be the first manifestation, though frequently the state of alcoholic tremulousness passes imperceptibly into it. There have usually been at least ten years of excessive drinking before the first attack.

The symptoms are florid. There is great restlessness and agitation. In the hospital ward the patient, weak as he is, may have to be restrained by two or more people before he can be got into bed. He is never still, tossing and turning restlessly, constantly engaged in conversation, switching from person to person, from subject to subject at the smallest stimulus and frequently shouting salutations and warnings to distant passers-by. His hands, grossly tremulous, clutch at the bedclothes; continously he tries to pick from them imaginary objects, shining silver coins, burning cigarettes, playing cards, or bed bugs. He is a prey to ever-changing visual hallucinations and may shield his face from menacing attacking objects, animals or men. At any moment his attention can be distracted by a chance gesture or remark made by someone round him. His pupils are frequently dilated and his ceaseless exertions have given him a rapid pulse and sometimes a fever.

He is completely disoriented. He may not know where he is, the time of day, the date or even the month. He misidentifies people, thinking for instance that the nurse is a waitress. At one moment he will fail to recognize familiar people, at another he will greet strangers as old friends, calling them by name and, if induced to do so, inventing the circumstances of their last meeting. He is intensely suggestible and readily responds to the promptings of his examiners so that, for example, he may be induced to tell the time from a blank circle if he is told that it is a clock. The patient is completely confused.

The prevailing mood is one of frightful apprehension which arises predominantly from his misperception and misrepresentation of his surroundings. He feels he is being threatened from all sides and that he must fight to ward off his attackers. But why does his mind react in this way? It is because the ego, the executive part of the self, cannot perform its functions when there is acute disorganization of the brain. The alcoholic has been coping with the sensed disapproval of other people for a long time and in his confused state now acts on fears and suspicions which he normally represses.

There is no need to inquire about hallucinations. Their presence is only too apparent. The patient responds to imaginary voices and reacts to imagined sights. He sees, in particular, rapidly moving small objects. Rats and mice are traditionally described but often the animals are far more threatening – big black flies buzzing at the face, cats coming to claw at him. Sometimes the hallucinations are more bizarre: 'Zip-fastening suitcases biting at my legs', said a recent patient. Sometimes the fear changes to resignation – 'I know you're going to kill me: get on with it.' Sometimes there are moments of bonhomous joviality when he will offer drinks all round; but it is not long before the fear reasserts itself. No words can do justice to the picture of fully developed delirium tremens during the hours or days before the patient falls exhausted into a deep sleep. He generally emerges from this little the worse and with his memory for the recent events mercifully blunted.

Unchecked, the condition usually takes three or four days to run its course but fortunately it can now be considerably modified by drugs. Deaths still occur, largely as a result of other illnesses present at the same time. Since the delirium is a withdrawal reaction we have to ask why the drinking was stopped. Usually this is because something made it impossible for the alcoholic to keep up his supply. Often a man is admitted to hospital with an illness, such as pneumonia, or with an injury following an accident. Unless it is realized that he is an alcoholic and, therefore, the possibility of his developing delirium tremens is anticipated, the subsequent enforced withdrawal of alcohol will not be compensated for by appropriate medication. About three days later the physician or surgeon will be presented with a case of delirium tremens. If the possibility is borne in mind, however, an attack can be averted completely.

Delirium tremens is correctly treated with large doses of tran-quillizing drugs such as chlorpromazine.

Alcoholic epilepsy, when it occurs, follows within a day or two of stopping drinking. Fits can be provoked in anybody, but the difference between the normal person and the epileptic is that, whereas the former needs a strong artificial stimulus, such as the injection of certain drugs, before he has a fit, the brain of the epileptic undergoes the requisite electrical discharge spontane-ously or with a minimal upset to trigger it off. The difference is essentially a quantitative one. The effect of alcohol (or, to be precise, of alcohol withdrawal) is to increase the susceptibility of the brain to undergo spontaneous electrical discharges re-sulting in fits. There may be single seizures or bursts. They are generally major convulsions in which consciousness is lost and they have to be managed in the same way as other forms of symptomatic epilepsy.

The knowledge that these states, alcoholic tremulousness, alcoholic epilepsy, and delirium tremens are phenomena re-sulting from alcoholic withdrawal is comparatively recent. Two pieces of research have been decisive; first, meticulous observa-tion of the timing of their onset in relation to the end of drink-ing and secondly the production of similar states following the sudden withdrawal of barbiturates.

Chronic alcoholics are likely to be deficient in vitamin B. This lack causes other mental disorders which are not the result of alcohol withdrawal. One is a severe disturbance of memory. In this state consciousness is not impaired and there is no confu-sion but the condition is commonly first noticed as an attack of delirium tremens is ending. The memory loss is selective and is best described in the account given in 1877 by the Russian psychiatrist Korsakov, by whose name *the amnestic syndrome* has long been called.

In these cases disorder of memory manifests itself in the form of a remarkably peculiar amnesia (memory loss) in which the memory

of recent events is disturbed, whereas long past events remain remembered quite well. Mostly the amnesia of this particular type
develops following prodromal agitation with confusion. This
agitation lasts several days, and then the patient becomes calm
again. His consciousness clears; he appears to be in better possession of his faculties; he receives information correctly, yet his
memory remains deeply affected. . . . On first contact with the
patient one may not note the presence of psychiatric disorder.
The patient impresses one as in possession of all his faculties; he
reasons perfectly well, makes correct deductions from given
propositions, jokes, plays chess or a game of cards; in short, com-
ports himself as a psychically normal person. Only after a long
conversation one may note that the patient confuses events, that
he remembers absolutely nothing of what happens around him.
He does not remember whether he had his dinner, or whether he
got out of bed. At times he forgets what occurred just an instant
ago. You have come into his room, conversed with him, and
stepped out for a moment. You return, and the patient has no
recollection that you have talked to him a moment ago. Persons
whom the patient learns to know only in the course of the disease,
e.g. his doctor or nurse, he cannot remember, and he assures
them that he sees them for the first time. However, he remembers
quite accurately past events which occurred before the illness.

It is almost unbelievable how short-lived the patient's
memory can be. One patient awoke each morning believing he
had been admitted to hospital during the previous night. Another, after weeks in the ward, still required to read the names
at the foot of each bed in order to find his own when returning
from the lavatory. Yet so well were his other faculties preserved
that, failing to remember investments, he had lost a fortune as a
stockbroker over the past few months without anyone realizing
he was ill. To compensate for the memory loss the patient con-
fabulates; he invents circumstances to fill the gaps and to cover
up. The doctor can readily induce such confabulations by suggestion. In addition to the memory loss, or perhaps because of
it, intelligence suffers. Problem-solving in both the actual and

the psychological test situation is not so well performed as formerly. Once the amnestic syndrome has developed it is not possible to reverse it completely though considerable recovery of memory may slowly occur with correct medication.

In another condition, *Wernicke's encephalopathy,* there is great difficulty in concentrating and slowness in answering questions although consciousness is full. It is frequently but not invariably associated with a memory loss of the Korsakov type. There is also a paralysis of some of the movements of the eyeball and frequently a disturbance of gait and balance. This condition is associated with pathological changes in particular areas in the base of the brain. It also is due to deficiency of vitamin B.

A number of chronic alcoholics show evidence of a continuing decline in intelligence as their drinking years progress. This is known as *alcoholic dementia.* Insidiously there is a falling off in their intellectual ability. They become less perceptive of what goes on around them, less capable of subtle evaluation of their experiences and they are handicapped in their ability to convey their meaning to others. New and complicated tasks seem harder to perform and consequently less inviting. They become duller. This is gradually perceived by their relatives and associates but is accepted as a behaviour change rather than as evidence of intellectual loss. Psychological tests reveal the true nature of this state because they provide evidence of organic impairment of intelligence. The condition is due to destruction of brain cells. When the impairment is gross the patient may be incapacitated and have to stay permanently in a psychiatric hospital. We know now that this is due to brain disease rather than, as Victorian moralists and physicians were wont to believe, an expression of moral degeneration. Dementia is by no means an inevitable consequence of chronic alcoholism. When present it is irreversible but the majority of chronic alcoholics who have been successfully treated are able to live full and energetic lives without any evidence of intellectual impairment.

All the foregoing conditions are unquestionably organic in
aetiology. They are caused by chemical or structural abnormalities in the brain. But other psychological conditions are found
which have not been shown to have an organic basis. These are
called 'functional' disorders. This name puts them in line with
the majority of psychoses unrelated to alcohol, and these they
in some measure resemble. There is still controversy whether,
when these conditions develop in an alcoholic, the drinking was
their cause or merely their first manifestation. Such doubts cannot be altogether resolved and it is wiser just to describe the
conditions rather than to attempt authoritative explanation.

The first of these is *pathological jealousy*. Generally affecting
men but sometimes women too, the jealousy is directed towards
the spouse, who is believed to be unfaithful. Pathological jealousy goes far beyond normal jealousy. Fleeting suspicions
which can be easily resisted are commonly described by
alcoholics; the wives may not be distressed by the observant
attention which their husbands give them. As jealousy becomes
more intense the alcoholic may still retain the ability to question
his suspicions, although these are now disturbing enough to
him to feature as a symptom (see page 101). In some cases belief
in the spouse's infidelity reaches delusional force. It may not be
overcome by reasoning, and resists clear-cut evidence which
rebuts specific allegations. The jealous husband seizes upon
any chance remark that his wife makes, any passing glance she
may receive from a man, to feed his suspicions. He searches her
handbag for letters and her clothing for tell-tale signs. Of
course, he disbelieves her protestations and frequently not only
upbraids her but beats her for her supposed adultery. Her lot
may become unbearable, yet so limited is the field of her husband's delusions and so rational is he in every other particular
that it is next to impossible to order his compulsory detention in hospital. Needless to say, he will not go voluntarily.
Separation is often the only practicable course, although its
immediate effect is to fan the flame of suspicion. Divorce courts

frequently hear testimony of pathological jealousy and it may result in murder. Why this condition should be particularly associated with alcoholism is a mystery. Psychoanalysts maintain that pathological jealousy is a manifestation of disguised homosexuality. It is a defence for the patient against the recognition of his own inclinations and at the same time, covertly, a gratification of them. He projects on to his wife his own unrecognized feelings for the other man. Once pathological jealousy has reached the stage of delusions the outlook for recovery is not good. Some patients develop an illness resembling schizophrenia. However, less extreme forms of jealousy commonly fade if the patient gives up drinking.

Another psychotic condition is *alcoholic hallucinosis*. The patient, who is fully conscious, hears voices which, characteristically, are talking about him in obscene language. The hallucinations may clear up if he stops drinking, but not necessarily; sometimes, even with abstinence, they continue for years. One patient, a bookmaker, described how he had been 'on the line' to such voices for ten years, during which time he had been able to continue working and drinking. When he gave it up they stopped but when he relapsed they returned and although he was subsequently enabled to remain teetotal they persisted. Auditory hallucinosis of this sort is quite different from the vivid, transient and disorganized hallucinations that occur with alcoholic tremulousness or with delirium tremens.

I clearly heard a conversation between my mother and my domestic help, which I thought was taking place outside the kitchen. Throughout the day, I frequently asked members of the household to repeat what they had just said as I had not heard it properly, only to be told that no one had uttered a word. I frequently heard my husband's voice calling me, as if he were upstairs or in the hall.

The next day I was defrosting my refrigerator when I distinctly heard my husband in his office, which is completely away from our house. I heard him having consultations with three different people, then dictating letters and talking to his secretary. It seemed to me that I was actually hearing what was happening at that precise moment.

During the early afternoon I was most disturbed to hear a strange male voice which was loud and clear, and claimed to be my conscience. By this time I was in a state of agitation; I sincerely believed this to be my conscience rebuking me. I was getting absolutely no peace from this voice, which was accompanied by music, and a mixed choir all of which had the quality of what I would call Church music. After the evening meal was over this became so loud and persistent that I felt anyone in the room with me could not fail to hear it as well as I was receiving it. Therefore I escaped by myself on every possible occasion and even found myself talking aloud in reply to this 'conscience'. My husband became very curious as to the reason for my frequent disappearances and, in the end, I took him into my confidence. As the evening wore on, the nature of the voice and music changed completely and became almost raucous. The voice introduced himself as 'Jimmy Young' from Glasgow, my home-town. I have never at any time in my life known anyone by this name. The tone of voice at times was very polished, but sometimes it assumed a very decided Glasgow accent. Gradually it became louder and louder, and almost mocking and jeering at me, to the extent that I became angry with myself for being so taken in as ever to believe this could be my conscience. I began to be convinced that this was some extraordinary type of radio wave which some cranks had been able to 'tune' in to me.

This patient recovered completely. Unfortunately not all patients do.

There is no evidence to incriminate any organic process. The condition of alcoholic hallucinosis is neither a withdrawal symptom nor due to a vitamin deficiency but is much more closely related to schizophrenia and, if it persists, it cannot be distinguished from that disease except by the history. Fortunately it is not common.

Chapter 4

SOCIAL ORGANIZATION AND DRINKING

THE study of primitive cultures sheds light on Western drinking. Anthropologists have frequently found that inferences can be drawn from simple cultures more readily than from complex ones, and that their conclusions then prove relevant to more differentiated societies. Only where the culture fosters drinking will alcoholism be widespread. Whatever the individual's psychological difficulties may be, unless the social circumstances are right he will deal with these in another way than by excessive drinking.

Favourable cultural conditions for promoting alcoholism must obviously include availability of supplies. But this by itself is not enough. From a sociological standpoint everybody may be regarded as potentially alcoholic; in Ullman's view, for instance, recourse to alcohol is no more than a means of relieving tension, and tension is universal.[1]

In simple cultures, where literacy does not exist, everyone has his place, with an importance and a dignity that the group recognizes. As social differentiation increases in complex cultures more rules are required. Those individuals who find themselves hard pressed to fulfil the requirements imposed on them become anxious because they must suppress and inhibit some of their urges in order to conform.

Rules check individual behaviour. As a society's rules become more complex, and especially where their enforcement is harsh and punitive, the individual has to limit the extent to which he can act solely in accord with his own wishes. In practice,

1. Ullman, A. D. (1962). 'First drinking experience as related to age and sex'. In *Society, Culture and Drinking Patterns*, ed. Pittman, D. J., and Snyder, C. R. New York: John Wiley & Sons.

restrictions are most stringent where they relate to aggressive and sexual behaviour. The threat of retaliatory punishment evokes anxiety in a person whenever sexual or hostile urges are aroused. Because these are vigorous urges, a powerful conflict situation is set up in the individual. From time to time recourse may be had to alcohol to facilitate release of these proscribed urges.

In very simple cultures drinking consolidates group cohesiveness and alcoholism is rare. The emotions aroused by alcohol are shared in the group setting and enhanced by singing and ritual. Drunkenness, too, is a shared behaviour. It takes the form of periodic revels; these enable the individuals to experience and express their close links with each other. In such societies anxiety and fear are significant not only as individual experiences but also as group phenomena. Horton, an anthropologist, records that the frequency with which drunkenness occurs in such societies is determined by the amount of anxiety and fear experienced by the group. In a study of 118 primitive cultures in Africa, Asia, and the Americas[1] he was able to relate the frequency of drunkenness to two indices of social anxiety: insecurity about food supplies and, secondly, stresses from acculturation by contact with Western civilization which weakened social patterns and kinship ties. The more these factors operated, the more drunkenness there was.

The combination of the group fears and the individuals' repressed urges becomes too great. Something has to give. These societies have evolved an adaptive pattern designed to relax their restraints from time to time. Popular festivities take place during which group drunkenness occurs. Then sexual and aggressive behaviour do not incur censure, and exposure, suggestive body movements and intercourse, arguments and brawls are permitted. Apart from these orgies drunkenness is rare and alcoholism does not occur.

1. Horton, D. (1943). 'The functions of alcohol in primitive societies: a cross-cultural study'. *Quarterly Journal of Studies on Alcohol*, 4, 199.

When the organization of society becomes still more complex, as in modern European societies, acting-out behaviour of this sort is no longer tolerated, even on the rare occasions when group drinking is still permitted. On such public days of celebration, although drunkenness is more excused than at other times, excesses of aggressive or sexual behaviour are not condoned. The excessive drinker in Western societies drinks *against* his society. Excessive drinking becomes almost a rebellious gesture. The conditions are right, the scene is now set, for some people to become alcoholics.

In different Western nations society has organized itself in diverse ways, and from country to country patterns both of drinking and of excessive drinking vary. Climate and geography, economics and local customs all influence national patterns of drinking.

The contrast between Italian and French drinking demonstrates well that differences in social attitudes play a very important part in determining the extent of alcoholism.

In France a third of the electorate gets all or part of its income from the production and sale of alcoholic drinks. These people are wholly or partly dependent on the wine and spirit industries for their livelihoods. In a quite literal sense they are supported by alcohol. It is understandable, therefore, that four fifths of French people replied, on being questioned, that wine was 'good for one's health' and a quarter held that it was indispensable.[1] Large quantities of alcohol are taken regularly by many Frenchmen without their considering that they are drinking too much or that they are misusing alcohol. Men who were asked the question how much wine a working man could drink daily 'without any inconvenience' gave answers which averaged two litres, slightly over three pints. The consumption of large quantities of wine was thought quite proper by the people surveyed. French drinkers consume wine steadily

1. Bastide, M. (1954). 'Une enquête sur l'opinion publique à l'égard de l'alcoolisme'. *Population* 9, 13.

throughout the day so that these inveterate drinkers constantly have a high amount of alcohol in their bodies. They are chronically poisoned, although they rarely show very disturbed behaviour. Their drinking becomes a problem principally because of the insidious physical consequences. They develop bodily rather than mental diseases. Indeed, French psychiatrists disagree among themselves whether alcoholism should be regarded as a psychiatric problem at all.

Italy, too, has a considerable economic stake in alcohol production. Ten per cent of arable land is under viticulture, more than in France. Two million people earn their living wholly or partly from the production or sale of wine. Drinking throughout the day, in particular drinking during working hours, has traditionally not been part of the *mores* of Italian society. Indeed it has been intensely disapproved. In 1958 it was reported[1] that less than a fifth of Italian men drank other than at meal times, and most of those only on infrequent, special occasions. More than a litre (1¾ pints) in a day was regarded as grossly excessive. Drinking took place in the family circle, and drunkenness was deplored. Consequently little alcoholism presented either to psychiatrists or to general physicians.

The difference in the extent of alcoholism in these two wine-producing countries has to be understood in terms of the different attitudes to excessive drinking and drunkenness which prevailed.

More recently a rising rate of alcoholism has been reported from Italy. Industrial workers, especially those who are single or separated, make up the majority; 96 per cent of alcoholics still drink mainly or only wine.

In Britain and in North America drinking takes a different pattern. It is neither continuous throughout the day, nor is alcohol taken exclusively with meals as a shared family activity. Furthermore, a large amount of spirits is drunk. Beer and

1. Lolli, G. E., Serianni, G. M. G. and Luzzatto-Fegiz, P. (1958). *Alcohol in Italian Culture*. Glencoe, Illinois: The Free Press.

spirits are the prevalent drinks in contrast to the wine of Continental countries. Moreover, drink is taken rapidly, either when work is finished or after the evening meal, to produce a sudden rise in the level of alcohol in the body. This method of drinking leads to drunkenness, which is the hallmark of Anglo-Saxon excessive drinking. The level of spirit drinking in Britain in 1963 was the highest for forty years. Every adult on average consumed four bottles in the year, two of which were whisky.[1]

Five types of establishment are licensed to sell drink for consumption on the premises in Britain: hotels, restaurants, public houses, bars, and registered clubs. Other places, off-licenses, and, in Scotland particularly, licensed grocers, are permitted to sell drink for consumption away from the premises. The pub is the principal *locus* of drinking in Britain. In England the public house provides drink in a pleasant and convivial social atmosphere; in many a piano is part of the setting; games, darts, dominoes, and the like are available; in most pubs women are welcome. Many pubs have their own darts teams which compete with rival houses. A man often becomes so attached to one pub that he does not lightly go elsewhere for his drink. Each pub has its band of regulars who feel at home in each other's company.

The encouragement of social activities is a comparatively recent development in English public houses. Tables and comfortable chairs are generally provided in the lounge, which has become the principal room. The publican frequently organizes entertainment on Friday and Saturday evenings. The old division into saloon and public bars is giving way as a result of a deliberate policy by the brewers (who own most public houses) to attract women into their establishments. A recent series of advertisements had as their slogan 'Let's all meet at the pub'; the accompanying pictures always showed equal numbers of men and women, thus indicating that the pub could and should

1. *Annual Report of the Commissioners of Customs and Excise, 1962–63.* London: H.M.S.O.

serve as a place for mixed social concourse. In Scotland the old pattern persists. Women are unwelcome; indeed some publicans contrive actively to discourage them. Many public houses in Scotland are still very much drinking shops whose customers are presumed not to want to do anything else. Few concessions are made to comfort: surroundings are dingy; seating is sparse and hard; ventilation is poor and sanitation woeful. Customers come to consume alcohol in a one-sex setting. The effects of this upon personal behaviour and group conduct have important implications for the development of alcoholism. The restraining influences of social conventions are weakened. Pathological drinking is more frequent in Scotland than in England.

For all its importance in British life the ways of the public house have received little attention from sociologists. Hopkinson in *The Pub and the People*[1] reports a survey by Mass Observation carried out during the war. Seebohm Rowntree and G. R. Lavers[2] give an account in *English Life and Leisure* which we cannot better:

The nature of any public house is largely determined by the locality in which it is situated, for that determines the type of customers, and the customers in turn determine the atmosphere of the house. Thus, in the centre of a large city, where there are practically no residents but only a heterogeneous crowd of passers-by, some of whom want a drink, public houses tend to be impersonal, 'cold', and often rather sordid. At the other extreme, in rural areas, and in some small towns and suburbs, public houses are not infrequently social institutions of considerable importance to the communal life of the neighbourhood. In between the two extremes there is an immense number of variations – 'tough' pubs in the docks, palatial houses complete with dining-rooms, usually in middle-class residential areas, public houses outside stations, catering mainly for travellers, public houses catering for factory

1. Hopkinson, T. (1945). *The Pub and the People*. London: Gollancz.
2. Seebohm Rowntree, B. and Lavers, G. R. (1951). *English Life and Leisure*. London: Longmans. Quoted by permission of the publishers.

workers or for white collar workers, or for both, in separate rooms of the same establishment, and so on. Broadly speaking there is somewhere a public house for almost every male taste. Taking public houses as a whole, their customers thus tend to be a cross-section of the male population.

Most public houses have a proportion of regular customers, varying from a small number in houses that cater mainly for passers-by to a high proportion in those houses that cater specifically for the requirements of one special locality, such as a village or a housing estate. Although the etiquette of town and country public houses varies a good deal, regular customers have much the same characteristics in both. They tend always to occupy the same seat or corner, and are annoyed if some other customer occupies it. They expect extra consideration, and minor privileges.

... the atmosphere of a public house is principally determined by its location and the type of persons from among whom, in consequence, it draws its customers, but whether a public house is a happy or friendly place, or the reverse, depends also largely on the publican and his assistants. It is strange that there should be so many morose publicans – only a minority, of course, but an appreciable minority.

A study by the Hulton Readership Survey[1] carried out since the war is the most up to date about British drinking habits. It showed that, of the population over the age of 16, 32 per cent were regular beer drinkers, 10 per cent were regular spirit drinkers and 5 per cent were regular wine drinkers. ('Regular' here means at least once a week.) The percentages of those who drank every day were: 9 per cent, beer drinkers; 1·5 per cent, spirit drinkers; 1 per cent, wine drinkers. 21·5 per cent of men and 40 per cent of women did not drink at all.

The number of people engaged in the drink industry in Britain is far from inconsiderable. Seebohm Rowntree and Lavers[2] made a very conservative estimate of 340,000. This

1. Hulton Readership Survey. Figures quoted by kind permission of The National Trade Press Ltd.
2. Seebohm Rowntree, B. and Lavers, G. R., op. cit.

figure did not include those engaged in the wholesale distribution of alcoholic liquor. To give perspective to this total they pointed out that it was approximately 50 per cent more than the number of workers engaged in all sections of the gas, water and electricity supply industries.

In the United States alcoholism is rightly recognized as a very serious public health problem. Social concern about alcoholism is much greater than in Britain. Yet on the other hand social attitudes towards drinking have been responsible for the magnitude of the problem. From its earliest Puritan days, organized American public opinion has never been able to come to terms with alcoholics, but has oscillated between severe condemnation and frankly vicarious admiration. In 1919 the United States introduced prohibition. The effect of this harsh measure remains a disputed matter but there is little doubt that inability to enforce it, together with waning popular support, united to make it fail.[1] Equally strong public attitudes in the United States led to the formation of the National Council on Alcoholism, and of Alcoholics Anonymous.

Alcoholism rates among Irish Americans are between two and three times higher than for any other national group;[2] the Irish had the highest rate of rejection from the U.S. army because of alcoholism during the Second World War. The greater liability of the Irish to alcoholism has been explained by Bales[3] in terms of the Irishman's close dependence on his mother, the father's position in the family being insignificant and weak. The Irish mother keeps her son emotionally dependent on her. The immaturity so fostered seems more congruous in Ireland but, suggests Bales, renders the Irishman in the United States

1. McCarthy, R. G. and Douglass, E. M. (1949). *Alcohol and Social Responsibility*. New York: Thomas Y. Crowell and Yale Plan Clinic.

2. Hyde, R. W., and Chisholm, R. M. (1944). 'Studies in medical sociology. III. The relation of mental disorder to race and nationality'. *New England Journal of Medicine, 231,* 612.

3. Bales, R. F. (1946). 'Cultural differences in rates of alcoholism'. *Quarterly Journal of Studies on Alcohol, 6,* 482.

poorly adapted to deal with the demands of adult life. By excessive drinking he seeks to allay the anxiety resulting from his inability to cope with the competitiveness of adult status. Furthermore he drinks in bars where women are excluded; in this all-male setting social controls are reduced.

A different immigrant group in the United States, the Italians, has a lower alcoholism rate than the national average. All the same, Lolli found it to be eight times as high as among Italians in Italy and the comparison is instructive. Changes in social attitudes and patterns of drinking account for it. As we have already seen, in Italy drinking accompanies meals and is mostly in the form of wine; but in the United States less than 10 per cent of second generation Italian immigrants drank exclusively with meals, and it was rare to find men who drank only wine. Intoxication occurred oftener than in Italy especially among women (males: 84 per cent of Italo-Americans compared with 60 per cent of Italians; females: 51 per cent compared with 16 per cent). These figures refer to the percentage of people who reported one or more episodes of intoxication. More striking was the fact that 20 per cent of Italo-American women reported five or more experiences of being intoxicated, compared with none of the Italian women. Lolli and his co-workers[1] who carried out this survey write: 'Their American cousins, adopting American familial, occupational and recreational customs, and drinking patterns, begin to lose the protection of the Italian drinking tradition, and demonstrate new drinking problems.'

Mormons will expel a member because of drinking, so it is interesting that among Mormon college students there is a high incidence of drinking to intoxication with socially harmful results. Their excessive drinking expresses a rebellion against cultural trends, church pressures in particular.[2] Methodists are

1. Lolli, G. E., Serianni, G. M. G. and Luzzatto-Fegiz, P., op. cit.
2. Straus, R. and Bacon, S. D. (1953). *Drinking in College*. New Haven: Yale University Press.

brought up in constant awareness of the evil consequences of drinking. Total abstinence is enjoined upon their members. Yet during their student days they had more drinking problems than either Jews or Episcopalians. It was found that those students who drank generally concealed the fact from their fathers.[1]

Jews have a low incidence of alcoholism. They number 15 per cent of the white population of New York State, but contribute only 1 per cent of all white first admissions to State mental hospitals with alcoholic psychoses.[2] This low rate has been explained on the basis that Jews have no taboos against the moderate use of alcoholic beverages, which indeed play an integral part in social and ceremonial activity. Drinking to excess has always been sternly disapproved by Jews. Because the outlet of normal social drinking is permitted and approved, Jews seeking to express their personal conflicts do not turn to excessive drinking.

Our review of drinking in more primitive cultures and our study of drinking habits in Western cultures both permit the same generalization. When a society approves drinking and tolerates drunkenness, whether all the time or on special occasions, then many people will drink to excess. Because they will not be doing anything proscribed, will not be acting anti-socially, they will feel no guilt. Consequently, psychological abnormalities will not frequently be found in the excessive drinkers. If, however, the society disapproves of drinking, it will be especially critical of those who drink to excess. The population of excessive drinkers will consist mainly of two groups: those who seek to rebel against the social group and those whose inner tensions are so great that they must obtain the relief afforded by alcohol, regardless of society's censure.

1. Skolnick, J. H. (1957). *The Stumbling Block*. Doctoral Dissertation, Yale University.

2. Malzberg, B. (1960). *The Alcoholic Psychosis*. Glencoe, Illinois: The Free Press.

These two groups are mostly maladjusted people with psychoneurosis or personality disorder. By their fellows, excessive drinkers are judged to be morally weak and self-indulgent. Being products of their society they share this estimate of themselves. They experience much guilt. The condemnation by society and their own sense of shame conspires to bring about their isolation.

HISTORICAL CHANGES IN DRINKING HABITS

The pattern of drinking in Britain has changed with modifications in the organization of society. Of the days of Queen Anne, Trevelyan[1] writes:

Drunkenness was the acknowledged national vice of Englishmen of all classes, though women were not accused of it. A movement for total abstinence was out of the question, in days before tea or coffee could be obtained in every home and when the supply of drinking water was often impure. But tracts in favour of temperate drinking were freely circulated by religious bodies and anxious patriots, setting forth with attractive detail the various and dreadful fates of drunkards, some killed attempting to ride home at night, others seized by a fit while blaspheming, all gone straight to Hell. Among the common folk, ale still reigned supreme; but ale had a new rival worse than itself in the deadly attraction of bad spirits. The acme of cheap spirit-drinking was not indeed reached till the reign of George II, in the days of Hogarth's 'Gin Lane', but things were already moving in that direction.

Meanwhile the upper class got drunk sometimes on ale and sometimes on wine. It is hard to say whether the men of fashion or the rural gentry were the worst soakers. But perhaps the outdoor exercise taken by the fox-hunting, sporting, and farming squire made him better able to absorb his nightly quantum of October, than the gamester and politician of St James's Square to escape the ill effects of endless Whig toasts in port and Tory toasts in

1. Trevelyan, G. M. (1944). *English Social History*. London: Longmans. Quoted by permission of the publishers.

French claret and champagne. Magistrates often appeared on the bench heated with wine; Court Martials, by a prudent provision of the Mutiny Act, might only take place before dinner.

The worst excesses of the gin palace era of cheap spirits were checked in 1751 by an Act which taxed them highly and stopped their retail sale by distillers and shopkeepers. Even after this, however, as many as an eighth of the deaths of London adults were attributed by medical men to excess in spirit-drinking.[1] Tea became a strong competitor to alcohol towards the end of the eighteenth century. The industrial revolution brought with it a resurgence of excessive drinking, particularly in the cities. Alcohol became for many the only recourse from the miseries inflicted by direst poverty. In the wake of this orgy of mass drinking the temperance movement grew up in the latter half of the nineteenth century. Doctors, clergyman and others not only urged the merits and indeed duties of temperance upon a largely heedless public but, more to the point, succeeded in producing in 1914 effective legislation licensing the places which could sell drink and fixing hours for its purchase and consumption. Trevelyan[1] comments:

When Queen Victoria died, drinking was still a great evil from the top to the bottom of society, more widely prevalent than in our day, but decidedly less than when she came to the throne.

These laws abated some of the worst excesses at the time when some of the widespread social misery was being reduced. The beneficial impact of the improved licensing laws was rapidly felt but the advantages of temperance were much slower to be appreciated. It was not until during and after the First World War that drunken behaviour began to be considered unacceptable in every walk of society. During the depression in the late twenties and early thirties there was once again an increase in drunkenness, which for a long time had moved in step with unemployment. However, gross public drunkenness,

1. Trevelyan, G. M., op. cit.

people lying paralytic in the streets, is now a rare sight in England although it can still be seen in parts of Scotland. In the 1950s a new phenomenon began to be apparent in Britain, teenage drunkenness, probably as a consequence of the increased affluence of this age group. The increase in drunkenness in the young is rightly causing serious concern.

Chapter 5

THE PERSONALITY OF ALCOHOLICS

PERSONALITY is complex. A part of it changes from day to day, with alterations in mood and as a response to events or to people; such variations are evanescent. A more enduring part of the personality is made up of beliefs and attitudes which are not readily alterable; this is the side of someone that other people describe when discussing him, and which he knows as himself. This part is capable only of very slow change as he takes on new responsibilities or undergoes great emotional experiences. An even deeper part of the personality contains the drives and motivations which give the self its impetus. Many psychologists consider this core to be immutable.

To an observer, an individual's personality is manifested by his behaviour; it consists of the total of his characteristic actions and reactions. Abnormality of personality consists of an excess or a lack of a quality, such as assertiveness, common to us all.

Intuitive appraisals of personality, such as we all make when summing people up, are very different from scientific assessments. In day-to-day life our own feelings enter into our judgements of personality. The psychologist aims to eliminate this subjective element. He may do so by isolating particular traits of personality, such as sociability or aggression, and measuring their degree in different people. Or he may consider the total personality of those people he studies, and attempt a systematic classification of them into recognized stereotypes.

We can study the personality of alcoholic patients but we cannot say how much our findings are applicable to all alcoholics since it is only a minority that get to be examined by a psychiatrist. There is no single alcoholic personality. Nevertheless psychiatrists dealing with alcoholics recognize characteristics which occur frequently, either alone or in combination and it is these which we shall now describe.

PERSONALITY PATTERNS OF ESTABLISHED ALCOHOLICS

The Immature Personality

Some people do not reach the level of emotional development appropriate to adulthood. Arrested development of an aspect of personality at any stage leads to immaturity of personality. Some adults, for instance, cannot detach themselves from their parents' home. Others are extremely self-centred, unable to feel tenderness towards anyone else; such people cannot form an intimate and stable relationship with another person. Still others have a childlike need for approval and admiration. There are others who show great promise at school but who subsequently fail to realize what had been hoped for them and what they had hoped for themselves. Such people are preoccupied with private nostalgic memories of what might have been, boasting about those few things they have actually accomplished. It is a characteristic of all these immature people that in spite of their obvious assets they live unproductively.

Many alcoholics had an unduly close relationship with their mothers. One woman patient got drunk and suddenly burst out: 'There is a heaven and we will be together again, mother – oh, how I want to die!' Such intense and persistent ties to the mother are more characteristic of male alcoholics and may remain prominent even when the alcoholism is in remission. A 47-year-old man, extremely cooperative in treatment, said in great distress that he had to confess that he had been deceiving the doctors for weeks; although he was not sure he was right to do so he wanted to correct the information he had given, namely that his mother had died of cancer. In fact she had died of drink. This was the first time he had brought himself to disclose her 'lapse'; he had never even told his wife.

I thought it unfair to her memory. But after a lot of thought, as the days passed, I thought I should tell the truth about her. I sincerely apologize, but I could not help myself. There were ten children before me in our family, and one after. I was nobody. But I got a lot of pleasure out of doing little things for my mother. When the children had all gone to bed she would sit by the fire. I would get out of bed and brush and comb her lovely long black hair for an hour. There must have been something soothing in this, as she thought it made her sleep better.

No other relationship that he had experienced in his life had been of such intensity.

The attachment to the mother can be still more extreme, a passion which can engulf the son so extravagantly that his life is entirely distorted by the prolonged dependence. A man who had had a few drinks before a group-treatment session and was therefore less guarded than usual, told his fellow alcoholics that he used always to drop in for a cup of coffee at his mother's house each morning on the way to work. He then burst forth that he hated his father. When he was five he had seen his father slap his mother's face. That had spoilt his life. He had 'toddled' from the house into a field, vowing never to forgive his father, whom he had hated ever since. That was why he drank: he would get himself drunk and then go to his parents' home expressly to rouse his father by his intoxicated state. It gratified him to make his father distressed and angry. 'Can you wonder I am still single?' he demanded. The other members tried to divert the conversation but he would have none of it. When he was a little lad, he said, at the time of the slap, he had vowed he would wait for his father to die and then look after his mother himself. The others exclaimed with surprise, but he repeated that he would never marry; instead he would devote himself to his mother.

Adults who have their energies bound up in obsolete relationships are only partially available for current experiences. They are bent on living out in the present a family myth which they conceived in childhood. Because the myth is personal and kept secret it cannot be influenced and corrected by real events. The dependent adult who clings, because of an inner, private logic, to an outworn parental relationship, often sustained in phantasy long after the parent is dead, suffers serious limitation in his present life, and cannot undertake the roles which his experiences in adulthood create for him. This sort of person turns to drink because his unreal phantasies of a golden relationship with a parent provide such a satisfying and nourishing world for him that the real world has nothing to offer of comparable value. When actual situations conflict with his phantasies he drinks, so as not to be aware of them; he escapes into a world where they do not penetrate. We have described his recourse to drink as though it were both conscious and deliberate, but this is not usually so. The phantasy world may perhaps be present only as a vague feeling-state. When drinking he lessens the tension of his conflict by permitting phantasy to predominate over a subdued reality.

The Self-Indulgent Personality

Children need help, protection, and affection while they are growing up but each of these can be overdone. When a child finds a task he has set himself too difficult he ought to be helped, but there are some parents who rush in with assistance before the child has employed his own resources and imagination. The child of over-protective parents, deprived of the satisfaction of discovery and personal achievement, gets alternative gratifications by insisting that everything be done for him as if he were still an infant. He fails to develop self-confidence or learn self-reliance. A child needs to be guarded from common dangers but some parents shield him from all possible hurt so that there is scarcely a thing he is allowed to do on his own if his mother can imagine the smallest risk. She wants to obviate discomfort of any sort; in case he might be unhappy she will not leave him with other children of his own age. As a result the child becomes fearful of separation from his mother and will never learn the social skills needed to mix easily with, be accepted by and enjoy the company of others of his own age. He will be socially clumsy.

Such people remain self-indulgent in adult life. They are unable to accept frustrations. They live for, expect, and must have easy and continuous gratification. To be thwarted is intolerably painful. They often eat a lot, chew sweets and smoke. All these activities have been viewed as expressions of a persisting infantile urge to find satisfactions akin to sucking. Drinking serves a similar end. Certainly there are alcoholics who actively *enjoy* drinking. Those who suppose that alcohol addiction is all misery are wrong. A journalist spoke of 'my long love affair with drink'. When the degree of intoxication is just right, these drinkers feel that they have 'reached the ceiling of my world', as one put it. For them, to drink is a celebration. Sybarites, they isolate the pleasurable parts of reality. When drinking they dim the lights, play music and even at times costume themselves. They are expansive and boastful: 'When I drink I become an admiral.' They strive for super-pleasure. Yet self-indulgence deprives them of self-control: regulation of behaviour becomes increasingly difficult to achieve. The joys derived from a drink are a synthetic gratification which the alcholic knows he has not earned. Perhaps this is why there is often a tinge of disappointment in his description: 'I get to the top of my world, but usually it wasn't what I really wanted.'

The self-indulgent alcoholic, therefore, drinks for two reasons. It reduces the personal discomforts which arise whenever his wishes are frustrated and it provides him with a gratification which is always available and dependable. He, of all alcoholics, is most likely to drift into alcoholism without realizing it. He takes to drink like a voluptuary.

The Person with Sexual Problems

People who are not well-adjusted sexually fall into three categories. Some have little sexual drive; such a man is unlikely to become alcoholic unless he marries a woman who interprets his apparent indifference as a personal slight. In that case he may turn to drink in an attempt to increase his ardour or to escape from his wife's and his own recriminations.

The second group of alcoholics with sexual problems are those whose sexual drives, though normally directed, cannot be realized because they have a fear of all dealings with the opposite sex. They may blush and feel uncomfortable in the presence of women; they find it difficult to carry on casual conversation and are daunted by the possibility of physical contact, petrified by the idea of intercourse. Some of these men express quite unreal notions about sexual activity. They may confide to the doctor ideas that sex is objectionable and that intercourse is unclean and leads to disease; or else they may romanticize sexual relations, maintaining that any physical contact sullies their purity. Another common rationalization is that intercourse is physically weakening. All these are unconscious devices hiding more basic fears of being harmed by intercourse or of proving impotent. Impotence is common among alcoholics, some of whom say they overcome it with drink. Certainly it may antedate the onset of drinking. A railwayman found that when he tried to have intercourse at 16 he was unable to have an erection. He became engaged at 24 but would not marry because after months of trying he remained impotent. Twelve years later he was still single, and considered his almost nightly masturbation as a type of sedative.

The third category comprises the sexual deviants. For them either the object of love is not a person of the opposite sex (we refer principally to homosexuals), or a person of the opposite sex is the love object but normal intercouse does not provide the sexual satisfaction. Sadists, fetishists, and voyeurs come under this head. After many interviews an alcoholic said:

Oh, there's no actual perversion, not to my knowledge. It's just that I have standards, a sort of sexual 'must'. I'm not satisfied unless they are met. They are necessary for me to have an erection. The main point is the short skirt and high heels. Also a small waist, being generally of slight build and dieting to that end; the use of make-up, eyebrow shaping, jewellery – no woollen underwear or anything like that. There's some suffering involved as well. The shoe that's difficult to walk in, too tight. The fact that the person may be cold by not wearing warm underwear. The imposition of dieting, going hungry to lose weight. I won't have an erection *because* these things are carried out, but if they're not there I'm dissatisfied. I say to my wife to wear terylene for underwear, to get a new foundation and diet more. For a time she wore size 5 shoes when she should buy 5½. Now she has refused everything. She feels she's made a chattel. She says she'll come back to me only if there are no fetishes.

Sexual deviants take alcohol either in the hope that drinking will help them to achieve satisfactory normal behaviour, or to relieve the shame many feel concerning their perverse practices.

Homosexuals are in a special case. It is always possible to go to a pub where drinking is still a male preserve. The homosexual finds the company of drinkers congenial. He is likely to meet other homosexuals among them. The exclusively male company and the disinhibiting factor in alchohol may temporarily bring out homosexual behaviour (not necessarily intercourse) in men who outside these circumstances are normally oriented sexually. Heterosexual men have sometimes awoken following a night's drinking to find themselves in bed with another man. These are people with a homosexual component to their personalities of which they are unaware. A man may so strenuously repress the homosexual side of himself that he is excessively vehement in denouncing homosexuals. A gentle and kindly alcoholic whose repressed homosexual qualities had long been apparent to his psychiatrist reported, 'I caught two Greeks having homosexual relations in the Army and I was successful in having them arrested.' A young divorced boilerman of a similar type said, 'I nearly killed a queer one day for trying something – I wrecked his flat.' Such a man after a number of psychiatric interviews sometimes confides that when uninhibited through drink he has responded to a homosexual approach. Others may suspect their ambivalent position in spite of their expression of distaste for homosexuals.

The Self-Punitive Personality

It is normal to have aggressive feelings when conditions warrant. In the family, children are gradually trained to express reactions of anger with a moderation making it socially acceptable. If parents admonish their children to oversuppress hostile feelings while they are growing up it can lead to a fear of expressing anger in adult life. The outwardly docile products of such upbringing, even though they possess the intellectual and personality endowments to advance themselves, may be exploited by more dominating colleagues at work, or may be disparaged by a relative or upbraided by a spouse without being able to respond with open anger to the provocations. The man who has to repress anger may at length be driven, by prolonged harsh treatment, to protest but he will castigate himself afterwards, overcome by anxiety that drastic retaliation might follow his spell of self-assertiveness. For the most part he subdues his aggression and seeks to relieve the resultant discomfort. Alcohol offers a method.

It is frequently chosen. The unassertive man we have described is aggressive when he is drunk; the hostile impulses habitually concealed under normal social conditions are released by the disinhibiting effect of alcohol. But that is not the reason why he drinks. He does so to relieve his inner tension. Before he achieves this peace, there is a stage in drinking when social controls are diminished, when intoxication dispels the timidity and caution which customarily confine him. The transformation can be astonishing. While in this state he will vilify, strike and destroy. He is usually aghast at himself next morning, when he wakes to his wife's disapproval and sees the damage he has done.

The Stressed Personality

These four personality profiles will be recognized by all who
come into contact with alcoholics either professionally or as
companions. However, some alcoholics do not belong to any
of these types. There are other people who drink excessively if
they are emotionally overtaxed and cannot resolve the stressful
situation by rational thinking. When a man can see only one
element in a conflict, the other element being outside his awareness, no effort of will can solve his difficulty. This is the model
for the development of neurosis and if he did not turn to drink
such a person might manifest a full-blown neurotic illness. In
this sense, alcoholism can represent an attempt to ward off a
psychological illness.

A company director drank whenever he was required to
speak up for himself. If he had to make a proposal at a board
meeting, or if he had to converse with a comparative stranger
at a dinner, he would experience anxiety as a vague pain in the
stomach. 'Like a bath running away' is how he described it. 'At
dinner parties,' he said, 'I'm absolutely hammering at myself
to get a flicker out, to think of something, but I just can't.' At
work when called to exert his authority and correct an employee
he was stifled by the disproportionate rage he feared he might
express. 'It's a curious thing to say, but I see red. My head gets
bigger. I really do think I see red. I feel as if I might fall down.
It distresses me that my position calls on me sometimes to
hound people, to keep them up to the mark.' He was excessively strict with himself and felt it wrong to do things just for
pleasure. So harshly did he judge himself that he was angry if
he overslept by five minutes. He regarded his alcoholism as
due to weak will.

That man was troubled by morbid unconscious phantasies.
In some cases stresses arise out of actual events which tax a man
beyond what he could be expected to bear. A patient told this
story:

I had a horror of alcohol. I didn't touch it until I got my wings in the Air Force. Then three of my friends were killed in the space of three days. The expectation of life seemed to me six weeks, so I decided to try drinking. I started to take a couple of whiskies in the evening. Within eight months I found that I could drink whisky as fast as other people in the squadron drank beer. I had quite a capacity. Throughout my service years I took a fair bucket.

He drank not only through fear but also with the thought that he should live as fully as he could in the few weeks of life remaining to him. He saw friends with severe burns and visualized himself similarly injured. For him alcohol heightened the joy of surviving each flying mission.

Drink is used as a medicine by people under stress. It does not serve as a tonic or as a sedative but as a pain-killer. With its help they can, temporarily at least, cope with their ordeals. Afterwards, when the stress is over, a man may get himself really drunk, this time to relax and unwind.

The categories of alcholic personalities which we have described are not mutually exclusive. Many alcoholics share characteristics of more than one type. Moreover, they are not the only types of personality seen among excessive drinkers; no personality is immune from alcoholism and any physician who sees a great deal of the problem knows patients who do not conform to these descriptions. Nevertheless, they are the commonest personalities to be met with, and we have tried to indicate the function that alcohol serves for each of them. To sum these up, we see that the psychological satisfactions of drinking are:

1. The lessening of frustration with increase in gratification.

2. The temporary attainment of a firmer social footing.

3. The release from social inhibition of important parts of the self which normally have to be kept repressed at great cost to the individual's self-integration.

T – c

People with any of the personality types we have described do not necessarily become alcoholics or even drink to excess. In fact it is a small minority who do. Drinking is only one possible recourse that they may adopt in order to come to terms with themselves or with others. These personality traits are common and though possession of them may prevent an individual from living his life as productively as he might otherwise do, they are not incompatible with a useful and ordered life.

We have described the personality types commonly found among established alcoholics and the function that alcohol serves for each of them. The psychiatrist cannot say with any certainty how much these personality types are the product and how much the cause of drinking. He dare not presume that the facets of personality which he observes were there before excessive drinking began for he knows that his patient has inevitably been altered by the effects of his drinking, not only physically but also psychologically and in his relationships with others.

Yet if we are seeking the causes of alcoholism, the reasons why people take to excessive drinking, the previous personality of the alcoholic becomes a matter of vital concern. What were they like before they began to drink? Although we cannot answer this directly from a study of people who are already alcoholics there are grounds for believing that the observed personality patterns were there before the alcoholism. In the first place, personality characteristics such as we have described are very slow to alter. Secondly, our patients who possess these personalities all seemed to have good *reasons* to drink excessively, reasons which were there before they became alcoholics. Drink, that is to say, appeared to offer a resolution of their immediate situational or inter-personal difficulties. Despite these cogent grounds, however, we must repeat that we can only make inferences about the previous personality of alcoholics. What is called for is examination, before they begin to drink excessively, of people who later develop alcoholism. Obviously this presents formidable difficulties but some attempts have been made.

Children of alcoholics have been studied and it is clear that alcoholics' sons, more than other boys, will become drinkers. These sons have been described as having 'passive-aggressive' personalities: an outward show of acquiescence and docility concealed strong inner feelings of anger and rebellion.[1] The suggestion has been made that the process of concealment or repression of hostility sets up strains; in time the psychological devices holding down the resentment become a burden, and these predisposed people become adults without ever having learned how to respond properly in anger-provoking situations.

Two hundred and twenty-five delinquent boys were studied in considerable detail in Somerville and Cambridge, U.S.A. and were carefully followed up twenty years later.[2] Twenty-four of them (11 per cent) were then recognized as 'alcoholic'. The authors' definition of an alcoholic was someone who had been referred to hospital for alcoholism, was known to social agencies as an alcoholic, had been a member of Alcoholics Anonymous or had been convicted at least once for public drunkenness. Compared with the other children they had, as boys, been outwardly self-confident and ostensibly seemed less troubled by morbid fears; they had been disapproving of their mothers and had no strong ties to their brothers and sisters. They had over-emphasized their independence. Yet later in life, as adults, many of them stood revealed as excessively dependent. By drinking it appeared that they satisfied their dependency needs while at the same time continuing to present a façade of masculinity.

1. Aronson, H. and Gilbert, A. (1963). 'Pre-adolescent sons of male alcoholics'. *Archives of General Psychiatry, 8,* 235.
2. McCord, W. and McCord, J. (1960). *Origins of Alcoholism*. Stanford: Stanford University Press.

Another investigation traced the subsequent careers of boys who had attended a child guidance clinic.[1] Alcoholism in subsequent life was found to be much more common among them than among a matched comparison group who had not been sent as children to psychiatrists. The children who later became alcoholic had been characterized by anti-social rather than neurotic behaviour. Their fathers had been inadequate parents, this inadequacy also taking the form of anti-social behaviour. The results of this study suggest that alcoholism may be the counterpart in later life of psychological troubles which had been present earlier.

These few studies are the only ones that have systematically examined alcoholics before they began to drink excessively. The evidence from them is not at variance with what we know of the personality of established alcoholics. Yet it is not enough to permit us to delineate a pre-alcoholic personality. Very varied types of people drink, go on to drink excessively and ultimately become alcoholic. We have recognized certain personality traits that are commonly found among their number but it is hardly possible to predict whether anyone who has not yet started to drink excessively is likely to do so in the future. Proneness to alcoholism is better recognized by studying someone's existing drinking habits than by assessment of his personality structure.

1. Robins, L. N., Bates, W. M. and O'Neal, P. (1962). 'Adult Drinking Problems of Former Problem Children'. In *Society, Culture and Drinking Patterns*, ed. Pittman, D. J. and Snyder, C. R. New York: John Wiley & Sons.

Chapter 6

CAUSES

In a search for the causes of alcoholism we need to consider: physical factors, including heredity; social and cultural factors; psychological and personality factors.

We have reviewed each of these areas and we can now try to draw the threads together.

Physical theories of causation

Despite a good deal of research into the subject no convincing evidence has been provided to make us believe that the future alcoholic is in some way marked out from his fellows by differences in anatomy, physiology, or pathology or by abnormalities of metabolism or of tissue chemistry.

Among the many theories that have been propounded on these lines, that of an allergic factor receives most attention because the members of Alcoholics Anonymous cleave to it. They contend that there is something in the physical make-up of an alcoholic – even before he has started to drink – which is responsible both for the craving for alcohol and for dependence upon it. This theory, which never found much support among psychiatrists, was convincingly rebutted by the work of Robinson and Voegtlin[1] who, after administering alcohol to alcoholics, found none of the characteristic reactions in the tissue fluids which characterize the allergic phenomenon; nor could they induce such responses in laboratory experiments on men or animals where everything was under the optimum condition for their production.

1. Robinson, M. W. and Voegtlin, W. L. (1952). 'Investigations of an allergic factor in alcohol addiction'. *Quarterly Journal of Studies on Alcohol, 13,* 196.

Endocrine factors have also been suggested but here again there is a lack of practical evidence to support the theoretical contentions.

Some workers adduce changes in brain structure. These, they claim, are early consequences of excessive drinking and, because brain substance is lost, they result in a lessening of control over future alcohol intake so that addiction can readily develop. However, it has always escaped demonstration that such changes do occur early in the course of excessive drinking. Several workers[1] have claimed to find X-ray evidence of loss of brain substance in young alcoholics and this, if it is confirmed, may make further study of the possibility worthwhile.

Nutritional factors have also been widely canvassed. One set of theories implies that certain individuals have a dietary lack of a specific factor (the N_1 factor) necessary for metabolism. Rats whose diets lacked this factor were found to take more alcohol than other rats. Later experimental work has cast considerable doubt on what may be concluded from such observations. Another theory is that alcoholics inherit an enzyme abnormality which, because it impairs metabolism of certain substances, increases the need for them and thus sets up a metabolic pattern predisposing to alcoholism. Although some of the research behind this theory has been carried out on alcoholics there is no warrant for the belief that any metabolic disorder is inherited or indeed that it preceded the alcoholism. This last objection applies to many theories which postulate physical factors operating *before* excessive drinking develops. Craving for alcohol, or dependence on it, has not been shown to occur before drinking has taken place, yet many of the theories require this for their substantiation.

Theories where the pathological or biochemical or endocrinological changes are presumed to be subsequent to heavy

1. Lemere, F. (1956). 'The nature and significance of brain damage from alcoholism'. *American Journal of Psychiatry*, *113*, 361.

drinking but then act to make it get out of control are more plausible. We have already seen that the setting-in of brain damage could be one such factor. There is no doubt that metabolic changes do occur consequent upon heavy drinking although evidence that such changes promote further drinking is still lacking. If it were forthcoming it would show that physical factors played a part in making the drinking take an addictive form but not that they led to excessive drinking in the first place.

The question of inheritance of a predisposition to alcoholism has been repeatedly raised. There is no doubt that it is a *familial* condition. Sons of alcoholics, for instance, have been shown to have a much higher incidence of alcoholism than other men of the same age.[1] But this transmission does not obey biological laws. It works by example. The father provides the son with a pattern of behaviour which he assimilates and on which he subsequently models his own adult behaviour. The alcoholism is passed on in the same way that money is inherited, not in the way that, say, eye colour is. Genetic inheritance of alcoholism has not been demonstrated.

Social and Cultural Theories of Causation

We have seen that cultural forces and social organization are both reflected in the amount of alcoholism present in a community. But to what extent are we justified in referring to such factors as causes? They act upon all the members of the community, yet only a minority of individuals become alcoholics. The impersonality of social and cultural forces makes it difficult for us to consider them as *sufficient* causes. And yet they are among the most important determinants of the size of the alcoholic population in a community. It becomes easier to see the causative nature of such factors if we consider the processes by which they operate. These fall principally into three categories – incitement, opportunity and example.

1. Nylander, I. (1960). 'The children of alcoholic fathers'. *Acta Paediatrica Scandinavica, 49,* supplement 121.

In conditions of full employment and high wages there will be a greater amount of leisure and people will have enough money to spend. With more time and more cash there is greater potential scope for drinking but when people use these assets wisely the level of alcoholism ought to fall. They are able to go farther afield, for more diverse pleasures, to the cinema, out in the car, to the seaside, instead of being restricted for their recreation to the public house.

Opportunity is another important factor and it is fostered by the way that society is organized. Supply is the parent of opportunity. Those whose work brings them into contact with alcohol have the highest rates for alcoholism and the alcoholic diseases. Publicans and barmen, waiters and others in the catering trade, brewers and distillers, coopers and draymen all have high rates. Alcoholism is the major occupational risk in such trades. (Does not the liquor industry in Scotland provide a likely explanation for the high rate of alcoholism there?) Other occupations also carry increased risk – officers in the Armed Services, actors and commercial travellers; each of these professions has a bar in the communal meeting place – indeed sometimes their meeting place *is* a bar.

Opportunity also accounts for the social-class factor in alcoholism. It is difficult to get accurate statistics about the social-class distribution of alcoholics because our best data, at the moment, are psychiatric hospital admission records and people in the professional and managerial class often make other provisions for hospitalization when this becomes necessary. But although mental hospital data *underestimate* alcoholism in the top social class this class still has the highest rate of admissions, followed next by social class II. Rates are much lower in the other three classes.

The number of outlets for drinking is another factor influencing opportunity. If there is a public house conveniently round the corner you are more likely to visit it than if it is a mile away. Of course, laws of supply and demand operate;

the more people there are who want to go to a pub, the more public houses will open. Nevertheless, opportunities for drinking in the poorer areas of our big cities were greatly facilitated by the generous provision of public houses in the town planning that accompanied the Industrial Revolution. In middle-class districts, however, and in the New Towns also, pubs are far less frequent. In France, it has been estimated[1] that there is one outlet for the sale of alcohol for every 45 inhabitants, men and women. By contrast it has recently been reported[2] that in Scotland there is one public house for every 80 men.

The most effective way to foster excessive drinking is by the power of example. The family is the chief agent. We have already noted how the child absorbs the example set him by his parents. If they consistently drink only in moderation, avoiding excess without effort, then the child is unlikely to become an alcoholic. But if, on the other hand, he often sees one of his parents the worse for drink then he will not develop the conventional social disapproval of drunkenness and will be more likely to permit himself to drink in a similar excessive way. At the other extreme, if his parents are rigid in their teetotalism, if he sees that they have been unable to come to terms with alcohol, then the child may in turn become fanatical in his own attitude to drink; should he also need to express rebellion against his parents he may become as fervently alcoholic as they were abstinent. That is why psychiatrists, when taking a history from an alcoholic patient, inquire as carefully for a history of teetotalism in the parents as they do for a history of alcoholism.

The power of example does not, of course, end when childhood does. Adults, too, model themselves on other people. If the young soldier sees his sergeants always with a glass in their

1. Mouchot, G. (1955). 'Letter from France'. *International Journal on Alcohol and Alcoholism, 1,* 75.

2. *The Times,* 30 April 1964.

hands he will seek to emulate them. If the teenager falls prey to advertisements which show sportsmen thriving on beer or suggest that girls appreciate the masculine qualities which, the posters proclaim, are evident in a drinker, then he will copy the image, thereby hoping to embody the prowess or the manliness.

Although we have separated these three modes of influence – incitement, opportunity, and example – we must note that they frequently overlap. Is advertising incitement or example? Is the availability of duty-free drink to the forces overseas opportunity or incitement? Is the heavy drinking in the officers' mess and ward-room example or opportunity? It does not matter. What is important is that by these means, one way or another, social and cultural forces exert a very powerful causative influence for the development of alcoholism. Equally, of course, appropriate influences can work strongly against excessive drinking. The organization of society can militate for or against a high rate of alcoholism. We discuss in Chapter 13 how the forces of society might be manipulated so as to prevent alcoholism.

The Relevance of Personality Structure

Unless the personality of the alcoholic is taken into account the development of his alcoholism cannot be understood. His addiction is meaningful only in the total context of his organization of beliefs, attitudes, dispositions and traits. His alcoholism is an integral aspect of the alcoholic; it is difficult to separate the man from the disease because so much of his energy and his actions are bound up in the addictive drinking and its consequences. Certain people appear predisposed to alcoholism by prior impairment in their personality structure. Such people exploit the gratification and the relief from tension conferred by drinking, because these psychic accompaniments of addictive drinking make their problems in living more tolerable.

People who use alcohol as a substitute gratification are those who are unable to get sufficient reward from ordinary living.

This inability stems from a faulty relationship of the ego to the rest of the self. Different schools of psychology have developed different ways of describing this. The terms and concepts used depend on the model of personality utilized. One of the systems most widely used is the psychoanalytic approach. In this, the growing individual as he passes through youth to maturity is constantly acquiring new patterns of behaviour. The progressive development of personality can be interfered with at any stage during this formative process. If severe interruptions in emotional growth occur, the personality does not evolve uniformly and to its mature form. It is deficient in some aspects and this deficiency reveals itself by a disturbed relation to other people. In psychoanalytic terminology, such a personality is said to have been partially 'fixated' at an earlier developmental stage. The stage will correspond to the age at which particular stress had been experienced. Under conditions of subsequent difficulty which resonate with the original stress, the adult individual can 'regress' and suddenly display, in the context of otherwise mature behaviour, his fixed immature reactions. These regressive actions or attitudes reflect preoccupations retained from much earlier periods in his life, in fact, the behaviour which was appropriate at the point in time when the original interruption took place. These aspects of the self had not shared in the subsequent maturation of the person.

This theory views the person as maturing in irregular steps. He retains residues of encapsulated feelings and impulses which, although usually latent, can suddenly gain an outlet in behaviour when fresh pressures occur. Then occurs an impulsive and inappropriate reaction, often surprising in its irrationality, as a response to the adult's present crisis. This seemingly incomprehensible behaviour becomes more understandable when regarded as the return of an unmatured childhood reaction pattern.

The socialization process by which all people develop starts in the parental home and extends through schooldays and adolescence, until in the late twenties maturity is reached. Disturbing experiences or emotional traumas are important because they can interrupt the continuity which makes up the meaningful life history of every person.

Very early experiences which the individual had forgotten can be revived in vivid detail. This has been done experimentally with the aid of hypnosis. The individual retains the impression of far more experiences than those he remembers consciously. Not only events but also the feelings that accompanied them are stored in memory and can be re-activated. The individual relives not just the happenings of past experience but the mood which accompanied the events. During psychotherapy it often happens that a patient recalls a forgotten occurrence, seemingly trivial perhaps, but a highly condensed and potent distillate of the past, which prompts him to remember experiences very significant for his development.

These experiences are aspects of the *historical* factors which play a part in personality. For the past determines current expectations, and these in turn influence the way in which one presents oneself to others. But current events, *situational* factors, also have important effects on emotional adjustment. They are the here-and-now experiences which trigger off disorganization of behaviour. A person may only partially comprehend such induced disturbance. It may be only a state of discomfort or anxiety that enters his awareness, and this may be the subjective tension that he seeks to relieve. Drinking may offer that relief.

The course of an individual's development consists of a sequence of new demands, each stage with its peculiar set of problems. The infant is a helpless being, entirely dependent on others. He progresses to the stage when social demands begin to be made of him. He has to comply in toilet training. Then, as he comes to participate increasingly as a member of the family, he has to master his anger when frustrated and to postpone the gratifications he longs for. He must control his jealous rivalries with brothers and sisters. He can anticipate the future and even see himself as a potential adult ('when I grow up . . .') with a sexual identification ('like my father'). The father is important in giving the boy a male pattern on the basis of which to evolve his own assertiveness; he also acts as a model with which the son can compare his own masculine behaviour in later adulthood.

In psychoanalytic theory, the stage of development at which major fixation occurred determines those infantile traits the adult will continue to manifest in situations which make him anxious. Oral, anal, and genital stages have been differentiated. An *oral personality* has tendencies to be passive, to cling to other people for support; though he is both demanding and grasping, he makes others his agents. He has failed adequately to master very early infantile impulses: these persist and find symbolic expression in excessive mouth activities and an urge to take things into the self. A relationship between strong oral residues in the personality and the genesis of alcoholism has often been asserted.[1]

The *anal* personality has developmental residues which show in maturity as excessive neatness, suppression of emotion, obstinacy and punctuality.

The *genital* personality is viewed as resulting from stresses later in development, at about five years of age; a person with emotional encapsulation at this fixation level is unduly preoccupied with sexual thoughts and impulses but at the same time keeps all relationships superficial and has little real capacity for intimacy. He or she tends to attract others sexually while simultaneously having to deny mature erotic needs and to repress sexual impulses. Men with a personality of this type generally have associations with numerous women but they are unable to form a stable and satisfying relationship with any one.

Many alcoholics manifest behaviour characteristic of the

1. Fenichel, O. (1945). *The Psychoanalytic Theory of Neurosis*. New York: Norton.

oral personality. Without being aware of it they are absorbed in mouth activities, and display passivity and dependency, together with a tendency to place excessive reliance on another person, usually of greater competence. This constellation of dependency features within the adult personality is accentuated when alcohol is taken; but it is also a persistent, hampering element that the alcoholic must contend with when he is not drinking. In a crisis he is apt to respond by adopting a state of helpless dependency. While the oral personality is the most common type found among alcoholics, there are also some who show anal or genital personality residues.

Fixation of development at the oral stage is often attributed to inadequate mothering, for example by a woman who is unable to provide adequate affection for her child. She may deprive her child of affection because she has to expend her emotional energies in another direction, such as going out to work; she may herself suffer from a character disorder or a psychiatric illness; if separation occurs, because of hospitalization, for instance, the child who is too young to grasp the true nature of his terrors may blame her for them and later in life hold her accountable. The relationship with the mother has much to do with the sense of security in later life. The oral personality seeks throughout life to find those maternal comforts which he lacked during infancy when they were so necessary for secure emotional growth.

On the other hand, the mother may pamper and anxiously over-protect the child. Knight[1] in studies of North American alcoholics reports that an overly indulgent mother plays a role in stimulating excessive dependency in her child; these patients commonly also had a father who behaved inconsistently, gratifying the child and then as arbitrarily reproving him. The adult from such a parental background has inordinate needs for affection, protection and care, and reacts with rage if not

1. Knight, R. P. (1937). 'The psychodynamics of chronic alcoholism'. *Journal of Nervous and Mental Diseases, 86*, 538.

gratified. Some alcoholics seek in marriage a mother substitute, and are likely to marry women older than themselves.

All clinicians who deal with alcoholics have been forcibly struck by the great amount of clear-cut emotional deprivation and trauma they have suffered. Alcoholic patients regularly describe the early death of a parent, parental quarrelling, broken homes, undue parental harshness and sometimes very gross cruelty or neglect. Alcoholics who have lost a parent early in life, or have grown up with parents who were psychologically disturbed or poorly adjusted to each other, show in their adult behaviour the effects of these gross traumas. The disturbing experiences which played a part in the genesis of distorted personality functioning, therefore, are not hard to find. The self-damaging attitudes of some alcoholics are clearly derived from relationships with their parents whose quarrelling between themselves often resulted in strife in the home. Patients are often well aware that the distress they experienced in childhood induced reactions which continue to disturb their adult adjustment.

The scheme of psychological development which we have outlined, with the theory of retention of residues of infantile patterns of behaviour, is of great value in understanding personality structure. The evolution and the current functioning of the alcoholic's personality help us to understand both the basis on which his alcoholism has developed and his behaviour during the course of drinking. We can now go further and perceive the effect of alcohol itself on personality function.

The three components of a person's psychological system are his *ego* (the conscious, realistically-directed, responsible self), his retained feeling residues of the *infantile self*, and his *conscience*, derived from the moral values of his parents. These three components must integrate with each other if behaviour is to be both appropriate and effective. Harmonious integration is dependent on the coordinated activity of the brain. But brain function is impaired by alcohol, so that even his precarious integration is lost to the alcoholic when he is drinking excessively.

Psychological concepts, although they clarify our understanding of the behaviour of an alcoholic by defining how the past is transferred to the present and influences a person's manner of dealing with current situations, cannot explain exactly why one individual and not another becomes an alcoholic. What they permit us to understand is which regressed personality aspects are allowed outward expression in the course of alcoholism, and why particular personalities are more prone than others to become addicted to alcohol.

Many and varied influences combine to generate alcoholism. There is no single cause. No one factor is sufficient by itself. Social, psychological and physical factors have all operated to produce the established alcoholic.

Chapter 7

VARIETIES OF DRINKING PATTERN

ALCOHOLICS' drinking patterns can take various forms which are quite different from each other. In this chapter we shall be discussing what types of drinking pattern we can recognize and the usefulness of distinguishing between them.

Some writers on alcoholism, particularly influenced by Alcoholics Anonymous, have tended to concentrate exclusively upon one pattern of drinking (which we shall be describing under the heading of the compulsive alcoholic) and to ignore the many other distinct forms that are to be found. So many of their members drink in this pattern that to them it is the paradigm of alcoholism. Jellinek[1] puts it: 'Alcoholics Anonymous have naturally created the picture of alcoholism in their own image'. This narrow approach does a serious disservice. It must be firmly realized that there are many people who have to be classified as alcoholics and need treatment on that basis, but who are not of the compulsive variety. Otherwise errors will be made both in the provision and planning of treatment services, and by turning away people who are motivated for treatment and would be eminently responsive.

A close examination of his drinking pattern makes possible much more than the mere recognition that a man is an alcoholic. Getting a careful account of the mode of drinking is essential for correct diagnosis and on this depends the treatment régime which will be advised.

1. Jellinek, E. M. (1960). *The Disease Concept of Alcoholism*. New Haven: Hillhouse Press.

THE UNSUSPECTING ALCOHOLIC

Some people drink themselves into alcoholism without perceiving that they are addicted. They may not have any conspicuous abnormality of personality. Sometimes, and this is far from being uncommon, a man will present with a physical illness or injury, the nature or circumstances of which prompt the doctor to question him about drinking. He may have broken his leg and appeared intoxicated at hospital; he may have a gastric ulcer or another condition to which alcohol is known to predispose; he may have one or more of the well recognized complications of alcoholism such as cirrhosis of the liver or peripheral neuritis. Questioning reveals three things: that he regularly consumes a great deal of alcohol, that he has never considered himself an alcoholic and that he has not before had any medical trouble from drinking. The physician or surgeon who views his task primarily as that of treating the physical disorder has grounds to diagnose the underlying alcoholism, but may be inclined to leave the interrogation there; the patient is then thought of as someone who is the victim of alcohol without being affected by alcoholism. Alternatively he may be recognized as an alcoholic but the management of this aspect of his condition is not pursued. The notion that he is an alcoholic or that he is dependent on alcohol he would vigorously dismiss if it were put to him. But it is not. The physician's disinclination to explore the diagnosis is strengthened if the patient does not show any craving for alcohol while he is being treated. Only if he asks for alcohol or shows withdrawal symptoms will the true nature of his dependence be apparent to all.

In our opinion, alcoholism developing by mischance, through long exposure but without predisposing factors in the personality, is extremely rare. Appropriate interviewing techniques will generally elicit from such patients first that if they do not have a drink their equanimity and poise is sufficiently disturbed to prevent them carrying on smoothly with life and, second, that there have been occasions when they have become fearful of the hold alcohol has gained on them, and tried to give it up. In spite of their protestations that on discharge they will effortlessly stop drinking, they seldom do so. Most of these people have insidiously become addicted to alcohol, but because they have acquired a high tolerance they have never appeared blatantly intoxicated. Consequently they may not come to medical notice until nutritional disorders develop, often hastened by dietary restrictions due to economic stringency. It is a great disservice to allow such people to leave hospital unacquainted with the reality of their situation. Occasionally one of them will manage to give up drinking by his own efforts but for the great majority special treatment is essential if they are not to continue to deteriorate. These people are addicted to alcohol. They cannot go for long without drinking once away from the sheltered environment that hospital provides. When they leave they revert to abnormal drinking.

An accountant of 40 was admitted to hospital with a gastric ulcer. At that time he was drinking two bottles of whisky a day. This was noted as a cause for his ulcer, and he was advised to cut down. When he was told why, he cheerfully assented. However, when he left hospital he found himself unable to do so. Eight months later he had an attack of delirium tremens. Even after this he could not accept that he was an alcoholic. It was only after a subsequent suicide attempt that he consented to enter hospital for the treatment of alcoholism. Evidence of a lifelong personality abnormality was then revealed. As a child if he was called on to perform at school or at parties he would weep. As a young man he could speak in public only if he drank beforehand. Towards his mother, and subsequently towards his wife, he was both excessively aggressive and abnormally dependent. In the therapeutic situation he at first attempted to evade exploration of his behaviour by adopting a manner of jaunty superficiality. When this was penetrated he became seriously involved in his own treatment.

THE REGULAR AND RESTRAINED ALCOHOLIC

We use this term to describe the alcoholic who must drink every day. His daily consumption may be considerable but he is not forced to finish all his supplies or to exhaust the money he has with him. To this extent, therefore, he is able to regulate his excessive drinking, and under the pressure of extraordinary social demands he may be able to take less than his normal wont. Nevertheless, he will not go for as long as a day without a drink and, as his condition progresses, he will always take a drink first thing in the morning. He cannot tolerate being sober but he rarely needs to drink to drunkenness. It is characteristic of this type of drinker that he can control the amount he takes in at any one time. This variety of alcoholism has been called by Jellinek 'inability to abstain'.

If he stops drinking, voluntarily or because he is obliged to, he will suffer craving and it is almost certain that withdrawal symptoms will appear. There is not only psychological dependence, therefore, but physical dependence also, the result of long continued excessive drinking. The patient has acquired tissue tolerance.

People who drink regularly in a group in a bar, with the same bunch of friends are a well-recognized variant. They compensate in this way for deficiencies in their social relationships. Everywhere else they feel inferior; only here, surrounded by trusted and uncritical companions, increasingly so as the evening proceeds, are they able to feel at ease, inspired by the fellow-feeling which the group engenders. Drinks succeed each other, round after round; each drinker orders in his turn, not only for the satisfaction of his own drink but also for the pleasure he gets from treating the friends he holds in such regard. Here, at least, he is somebody's peer.

Some who drink in this way are basically isolated, friendless people. Passive, good-natured, unambitious, they have never learned to form mature relationships and in the undemanding, casual camaraderie of the bar they are never taxed intellectually or emotionally; they are in their element.

These drinkers regularly consume a considerable quantity of alcohol in the course of an evening, yet because they do not hurry over it, and because they have had many years to acquire tolerance, they rarely show gross intoxication.

Gregarious drinkers are there for all to see. Equally so are some solitary drinkers. It is common in public houses to find men sitting by themselves at a table or at a corner of the bar steadily drinking hour after hour and clearly disinclined to engage or be engaged in any social intercourse. Morose, unheeding of their surroundings, they are conducting the business of drinking without the interference of conversation. They choose to drink in the pub rather than at home because they escape the family's antagonism and because the pub is geared to dispense their supplies with the minimum of inconvenience.

Other solitary drinkers drink at home. If they are women they will generally do this in secret. The woman alcoholic finds that social conventions do not allow her to obtain the drink she needs without some subterfuge. That is why she hoards and, indeed, why she drinks alone. Home drinkers generally drink every day. They cannot abstain longer. But the quantity stays under control. They do not get drunk. Women often make a pathetic attempt each evening to hide the evidence of drinking, both upon themselves and in the neglect of their homes, before their husbands return from work.

THE COMPULSIVE ALCOHOLIC

A different variety of alcoholism is that occurring in people who, once they have started to drink, cannot stop but must go on until all their money is spent or their supplies are finished or until accident or unconsciousness supervene. Such drinkers can have abstinent periods but as soon as they begin to drink again they cannot limit the quantity. This pattern has been aptly named 'loss of control'. In mild cases the amount of drink taken may gradually increase for several days after a period of abstinence. Eventually, however, even in these cases drunkenness is reached.

Another variant, which stops short of the full picture, occurs when some social self-restraint can operate although drunkenness has been reached; the alcoholic retains sufficient foresight and manages to desist in spite of there being drink still available. A married schoolteacher of 45 worked for five days each week without drinking. Every Friday as soon as school ended she would start drinking gin to such an extent that by nightfall she was very intoxicated, very outgoing and talking excessively. She misbehaved socially and abused her husband, accusing him of paying her too little attention. Next morning she would be unaware of the disturbance she had caused in her own and her friends' homes. She continued to drink during Saturday and became drunk and forgetful once more; on Sunday morning she would wake feeling remorseful and apprehensive and although she began to drink straight away she did not let herself get quite drunk. By Monday morning she was able to go to school and do her work for the ensuing week. She was more fortunate than most of those who suffer from loss of control. They are powerless to prevent their spells from going on to prolonged drunkenness. Invariably they suffer from withdrawal symptoms, for they have become physiologically dependent on alcohol and it is very common for them not to be able to remember the later events of the spell of drinking even though they did not lose consciousness.

Compulsive alcoholics are the mainstay of Alcoholics Anonymous. It is easy to see how they have developed the idea that alcohol is a specific poison for them on the basis of a prior physical sensitivity. The view is incorrect; but, since the alcoholic later becomes physiologically dependent, his idea that alcohol is a poison may fairly sustain him in his struggle for abstinence.

Between crescendos of drinking the compulsive alcoholic may remain abstinent for periods of some days. A stranger meeting him at such a time would not credit that he was an alcohol addict. Although this type of alcoholic finds temporary sobriety bearable, as soon as he has one drink a train of events is set in motion. He is compelled to continue drinking until his physical reactions, some serious disease or injury, or his mounting terror of the consequences if he continues, force him to stop. The alcoholic caught up in this furious progress can no longer choose between leaving off or continuing to drink.

The alcoholic who drinks in this pattern gets himself into serious social difficulties. His drunken behaviour repels. He alienates and antagonizes those who come into contact with him, relatives, friends and workmates, even when they are anxious to be helpful to him.

THE NEUROTIC ALCOHOLIC

The alcoholics described so far in this chapter were not suffering from additional clear-cut psychological illness. But alcoholism can be the most evident disturbance in a patient whose principal disorder is, in fact, neurosis. The alcoholism is not primary and the form of the drinking is not distinctive. Very varied patterns are adopted. Alcoholics with neurosis drink to reduce their subjective distress, to diminish their emotional conflicts. Their drinking represents an attempt at cure of the symptoms of the underlying condition. However, as it usually exceeds what is acceptable socially, it worsens their inter-personal situation. They use alcohol to try to counteract their symptoms which stem from disturbed inter-personal relationships, but unfortunately their friends and relatives have to put up with the added embarrassments of the drinking superimposed on the pre-existing psychological difficulties. So the drinking is self-defeating. Yet they may persist in it for many years, knowing no alternative. Physical dependence develops in time, with result-ant addiction. However, if proper attention is paid to the underlying psychological disorder the alcoholism may be relinquished by the patient. The treatment in such a case must aim to deal with the psychological disorder, but proper thera-peutic contact with the patient is not possible until the drinking has been interrupted.

SYMPTOMATIC ALCOHOLISM

Sometimes alcoholism occurs in a patient already suffering from a severe psychiatric disorder. This must then take first place in management. Alcoholism can be the symptom which brings to notice people suffering from depression or schizo-phrenia, from psychiatric illness due to brain disease or from mental subnormality.

The physician who treats numbers of alcoholics will always be vigilant to detect the patient whose drinking should properly be regarded only as a symptom of severe underlying psychi-atric illness, the diagnosis of which calls for careful history-taking and psychiatric examination.

A 60-year-old unmarried business woman was now retired. For forty years she had cared for her mother whom she described as a very determined person, the decision-maker in the family despite her constant laziness. In addition to being selfish, the mother distressed the family by always wanting to be at whist-drives, parties or the theatre. She had been widowed early and in her old age was deteriorated mentally; she had bowel trouble and soiled in the house. Six months previously her daughter, the patient, got down in the dumps, felt unable to relax and slept poorly; she did not know what to do about her mother and resentfully thought that the old lady just did not care about controlling her bowel movements. She began to drink heavily, soon taking half a bottle of brandy every day and a good deal of sherry. The drink did not relieve her depression but gave her the necessary energy to attack the added washing as well as the household chores. A month before she was first seen for her alcoholism the family doctor arranged for her mother to enter a home. The patient became still more depressed. She felt like a lost soul, increasingly sad and sleepless. She realized that she could not stop drinking. 'I think I'm an alcoholic. I don't think I'll be able to control my drinking even if I get better from this depression. Everybody says I shouldn't feel guilty about putting my mother away but I should have been able to cope until she was finished. It's duty rather than love.' She had used alcohol to boost herself up, to help her get some sleep, to reduce her restlessness and to ease the distress of 'worrying too much about things I needn't worry about.'

This patient's illness was a depressive reaction originally centred round her resentment towards her mother; her sense of failure and self-blame when her mother had to be sent away were other symptoms of the illness. The alcoholism was secondary to the psychiatric disorder. Drug treatment for her depression with psychotherapeutic measures were successful. She recovered quickly and proceeded to arrange a long cruise for herself. Drinking was no longer a problem to her.

Alcoholism may also be seen occasionally as an early manifestation of the psychoses caused by syphilis of the brain (general paresis), brain tumours or as part of the general picture of senile mental deterioration. In this group with structural brain lesions, the drinking tends to be both purposeless and poorly organized.

BOUT DRINKERS

We have left to the last an unusual drinking pattern which is not classifiable into any of the previous groups.

There are people who for three or six months, and sometimes longer, drink only socially, if at all. They then suddenly start to drink excessively, for days on end, drinking all the time, neglecting all their responsibilities at work or to their families. Sometimes they do serious damage to themselves or to others during the bouts. Days or weeks later they just as suddenly stop.

A 45-year-old male schoolteacher drank excessively in bouts of two to three days, with approximately four months between. The longest time between bouts was fourteen months.

Ordinarily I never have more than a sherry. Once I start drinking more, just civilized social drinking, it brings the possibility of a bout nearer reality. I know when one is imminent. I think to myself, 'I'm going to get drunk tonight and, God, how I dread it.' When I start up, there seems to be a determined attitude to get really stinko, plastered. I'm determined then to stay drunk for forty-eight hours to three days, until I get into a thoroughly toxic state. All that will keep me quiet is more alcohol. Only drugs can get me out of the cycle, which I badly want to come to an end. I've never lost a job, but I've had to be hospitalized a number of times. It's almost as if a bout is unconsciously planned. It happens when I feel: 'Now I can let go, escape from things.' First there's the build-up, then the letting go. I have a spurt of 'you only live once, to hell with it'. It's a wild, exuberant, thoughtless, throw-it-down. I weep for my wife in many respects. I honestly don't know what the solution is. I don't know what to do about myself now.

For many months a bout drinker may be untroubled by any urge to drink and, in fact, may have been able to drink socially; but once the bout starts it progresses relentlessly. A shopkeeper was seen after he had suffered from periodic drinking bouts for thirty years. He came for treatment because he felt that he could no longer bear the physical consequences of a drinking bout.

I get jittery, especially when I am trying to stop. What annoys me is that I can last for as long as ten months, but then it all starts up again. First I have an urge to start for two or three days, set off by fortuitous happenings, a drink advertisement which catches my eye or a brewery wagon passing. Then I succumb. I feel guilty about it soon after I have started, because I am a disgrace to my family. My daughter ignores me lately and she comes home late from school because she is sick of the sight of me; she wants to stay out of the house as much as possible rather than face the sight of me.

The great interest of bout drinking stems from this alternation of brief but grossly pathological drinking with long phases of normality. Periodic drinkers of this sort usually deny that any particular psychological stress is required to trigger off the drinking phases, nor can upsetting events be incriminated. This unusual form of drinking used to be called dipsomania or periodic alcoholism.

We have seen that the various patterns of abnormal drinking can be associated with disorders of personality (most cases come in this category), with underlying neurotic illness or with psychoses or underlying brain disease. Each of these characteristically sets up its own form of pathological use of alcohol and each requires a separate method of management. The global term of alcoholism is used to cover them all. But psychiatrists carry out a careful process of differentiation to determine the category in which a particular person belongs.

Chapter 8

STAGES IN BEING AN ALCOHOLIC

EACH alcoholic has his own history. Personal experiences, psychological disturbances, social shifts and upheavals, physical illnesses and changes in drinking habits all make their contribution to a sequence of events unique for each individual. But the student of alcoholism, who meets similar phenomena over and over again in different patients, discerns a customary progression. The alcoholic's total career spans successive periods of illness each with its own phases which can be identified by their characteristic symptoms as they proceed. Some events generally take place early; others feature in the late stages of the disease. The order in which we shall describe them is derived from considering large numbers of alcoholics; no particular patient will be found who follows it exactly. Events which typically occur early in the course may be found late in the histories of some alcoholics; or they may never be seen at all. Some patients pass with dramatic rapidity from the early stages of alcoholism to the severest levels with scarcely any intermediate phase. There are individual variations of considerable magnitude. The ensuing outline of a step-like series of phases represents only a composite picture; nevertheless it is faithful to the generality of alcoholics. The alcoholic begins with excessive drinking, moves into the addictive stage, and progresses to reach the stage of chronic alcoholism with physical and mental breakdown. Two transitions have special significance. They are points of no return. The first of these, which marks the onset of alcoholism, occurs when a person is no longer just an excessive drinker but has become addicted. The second, when he passes into chronic alcoholism, is marked by the development of severe and persistent bodily changes.

EXCESSIVE DRINKING

In the early stages of his abnormal drinking, although the excessive drinker takes more alcohol than the normal social drinker, he drinks in the same pattern. There are nevertheless warning signs that excessive drinking has developed. Not only is he drinking more than other people; he is, and this is very important, drinking more than he himself did formerly. He is *spending more time drinking*, more nights of the week and more hours each night. It may not be long before he finds that he cannot get enough by drinking in a socially accepted manner and he begins *sneaking drinks*. He drinks round for round with his friends but he also sees to it that he gets additional drinks between the rounds.

He *adopts stratagems* to get still more drink while disguising this from others. He may leave his companions for a moment on some pretext and have a quick drink in a different bar. Or he may go from bar to bar in succession so that the acquaintance he meets in any one will not realize the amount he is taking. At home, the pale liquid in his own glass may be whisky and not the sherry he has poured for everybody else. His visits to the kitchen are not always to get ice. In other people's houses he will not be long in discovering where the strong drink can be found nor will he be backward in pouring his own. He will have had a number of preparatory drinks before arriving at his host's and if he calculates that there will not be enough drink for him there he will bring along some of his own.

All these devices manifest his *avidity for alcohol* and his determination to get the quantity which he now requires. This he will do without shame because he is not yet aware what these actions portend. He does not see he is marked out from his fellows even though he feels the necessity of concealing his drinking from his friends in case they are beginning to notice.

Drinking at this stage affords him positive relief. He has

Phases in Alcoholism

STAGE OF EXCESSIVE DRINKING

More time spent in social drinking
Drinks more nights of the week
Sneaks drinks
Takes stronger drinks than companions
Adopts strategies to get more drinks
Preoccupied with drinking
Drinks to get relief from tension
Increased tolerance
Guilt over drinking
Social failures excused to himself and to others with
fabricated explanations
Needs drinks to perform adequately at work or socially
Feels drink has become a necessity
Increased guilt feelings

STAGE OF ALCOHOL ADDICTION

Onset of alcohol amnesias (memory losses)
Greater frequency of amnesias
Loss of control – compulsive drinking
Reduction in interests
Drop in work efficiency
Absenteeism
Drunk in the daytime
Reproof from employer or relatives
Low self-esteem
Remorse
Compensatory bragging and generosity
Financial extravagance
Deceives family, debts made
Increasing social isolation
Aggressive outbursts
Wife takes over more responsibilities

STAGE OF ALCOHOL ADDICTION

Deterioration in relations with wife
Paranoid misinterpretations
Self-pity
Justifies drinking with self-deceptions
Reduction of sexual drive
Morbid jealousy
Drunk at week-ends
Loss of job
Break-up of family
Morning tremulousness
Morning drinking
Conceals supplies of liquor
Repeated attempts to stop drinking
Suicidal impulses and attempts
Neglect of meals

STAGE OF CHRONIC ALCOHOLISM

Physical and mental symptoms dominate
Loss of appetite, poor food intake
Continuous drinking
Tolerance diminishes
Prolonged confused thinking
Use of cheap wines and methylated spirits
Delirium tremens
Goes to AA or seeks medical treatment
Serious physical diseases

discovered that the taking of alcohol lessens the tension within him. 'I was shy at dances and had a drink to relax me and make me more sociable. It gave me the courage to dance. I could not have done it without drink.' He feels better for drinking. A housewife may realize that she can entertain her friends, carrying out the functions of a hostess, without anxiety if she has had a few drinks. Having *discovered that alcohol brings relief* the excessive drinker now uses it for this end nearly every day. He has become a regular drinker.

This increase in drinking results in an *increased tolerance* for alcohol so that a given amount of drink affects him less than it did formerly. Although he has to drink more to obtain the relief he seeks, he may be quite cheered by this. He can take the amount he now needs and yet stay fairly sober. He may even congratulate himself upon his ability to hold his liquor. What is taking place, however, is a physiological change, an alteration in the body's reaction to alcohol. Round about this time he will take the first two or three *drinks with great rapidity* in order to get the effect as quickly as possible. He begins to feel himself different from other people, separate from his friends whose unspoken objections he senses. Certain of his friends he will deliberately avoid, cutting off contact with those whose criticisms distress him most. Paradoxically, this is part of an uphill and losing attempt to preserve himself socially by remaining only in the company of those who are not concerned about him because they are less closely associated personally. He invents explanations to excuse himself for missed appointments and unfulfilled promises and he dislikes himself for doing so. He knows now that he is covering up. He is beginning to be *assailed by guilt* about what he is having to do in order to get the drink he needs.

He has entered the stage of feeling that he imperatively needs the effects induced by alcohol to function effectively. He will expressly have a drink beforehand to fit himself for routine activities.

ALCOHOL ADDICTION

Drinking is now a necessity. He is taking alcohol for its effects. He frequently *drinks to the point of drunkenness*. Inevitably this has its physical consequences. *Losses of memory occur*. On recovery from a drinking session the alcoholic finds he has no memory for its later stages. He cannot say how he got home, nor can he remember whether he disgraced himself. In point of fact, his behaviour has generally been unexceptionable. The first intimation to his friends may be his anxious and devious probing next day to discover how he had acted. Lack of awareness during the drinking is not responsible for the blank; the appropriateness of his behaviour at the time proves this. He cannot later recall what transpired because no record of the events was stored in his memory. It is no use cudgelling his brains to remember; there is no imprint there to be recalled.

Patients drinking excessively are sometimes too shocked at the first occurrence of an amnesia to admit to themselves that a whole time sequence of experience had not been remembered. One described how disconcerted he was at receiving a letter from a business associate, dealing with a telephone conversation this man had had with the patient. 'I can remember no such conversation. I'm a bit worried that I may have forgotten. But I doubt that. Perhaps it was a mythical telephone conversation that he was referring to.'

Such memory blanks may occur in excessive drinkers even at times when they have not been drinking heavily. Some patients can tell you accurately when they first started. 'By then I would have a couple of drinks during the day and really hit it at night. I often awoke in the morning unable to remember what had happened during parts of the previous day.' Almost all can remember their first episode even if they cannot date it. Amnesic spells are particularly alarming if the patient fears that he might have done someone serious harm and be unaware of it. This happened to a young machine operator. His wife said that one night he came in late in a very distressed state and with blood on his hands and shirt and underclothes. He was unable to remember where he had been and what he had been doing. Later he made inquiries and he discovered that a girl at work had left the factory with him and they had had sexual intercourse. It might have taken place, he thought, in a forest or park.

The term 'blackout' is often used to describe this amnesia, particularly by alcoholics themselves, but it is misleading because there has been no unconsciousness. The abnormality is a failure to register events in the memory. Physical changes in brain activity are responsible for this extraordinary phenomenon. Upon the alcoholic the effect is shattering. He can no longer hide from himself that he is being harmed by drink. Many alcoholics seek help when experiencing blackouts at this stage of drinking. Nearly all alcoholics have had them. To the physician they are a clear sign that there cannot be a reversion to moderate, controlled drinking. The addict is set on an inexorable downhill course. When the *frequency of amnesias increases* so that memory blanks become quite regular and they occur not as isolated and shocking events but as repeated aspects of his drinking life, another milestone has been reached.

Once the addict begins to have no power either to decide in advance how much he will drink or to stick to that decision, he has *lost the capacity to regulate his drinking*. He finds himself repeatedly in the position of taking more than he meant to; the quantity he drinks is no longer determined by his intentions. This phenomenon is designated by the phrase 'loss of control'. The alcoholic has become a compulsive drinker. One drink leads inevitably to a succession of others despite the extreme inappropriateness of such behaviour. At its worst, this loss in control means that each time the alcoholic starts to drink he will go on until he is helpless.

His *interests become narrower*. Drinking takes up the greater part of his time, his thoughts and his energy. An evening at the cinema is an evening's drinking lost. He loses his friends and he loses his interests. His employer may first of all have noticed a *loss of working efficiency*: errors creep in, sales go down; unpunctuality and short periods of *absenteeism* occur. (In firms which seek to identify and treat alcoholics, works managers are taught to recognize Monday-morning absenteeism as a likely sign of alcoholism.) Even when he is at work, the alcohol addict may be inattentive, and forgetfulness may have serious consequences. Inevitably there will come a day when at work he is clearly the worse for drink. He has begun to be *drunk in the daytime*. 'I wasn't sober for the last five months of my army service' was how an ex-soldier described the occurrence of such daytime drunkenness.

All those with whom he has contact, relatives, friends, workmates, employers are remonstrating with him or reprimanding him. They warn him that unless he mends his ways they will take action. These *increasing social pressures* may make the alcoholic's position more insecure and exacerbate his drinking.

His self-esteem at this stage is very low. He regards himself as worthless and despicable. He may be tempted to misdemeanour by his overriding need for drink.

At first I'd go to the cash-box only to take change, to put a five-pound note in and take five single pounds out. Then I began taking money out to spend on drink, with the idea of replacing it on pay-day. Lately, replacing the money was my last consideration.

He is *beset with remorse* at the way he has let himself and everyone else down. To compensate, he may *dwell on past achievements*, sometimes exaggerating them in a grandiose way to impress those who are still prepared to tolerate his company. He may tell gross lies to put himself in a better light.

When I first met my wife I told her my right hand was weak because of a war injury. Really it was due to polio. I also told her I was five years older than my true age. After telling these lies I was obsessed with the idea that my wife might discover about the polio and leave me or that her father might ask me a question about the war and make my lies apparent.

To lend credibility to his tales of worthiness and success he may *spend large sums of money* in treating others with undue ostentation. It is not uncommon for a man to walk into a pub with a full week's wages and leave penniless later in the evening.

He may attempt to recover his losses by ill-judged speculations and he will frequently resort to gambling in a despairing attempt to recover his position and to improve his family's attitude to him. Of course it has the opposite effect. He may keep a mounting portion of his income for 'pocket money' or, if they budget that way, his wife may discover that her monthly allowance has not been paid into her account. Even more distressing is when she finds out that payments he was responsible for, hire purchase or building society instalments, for instance, have not been made. He has been deceiving her. From her point of view she is forced to the recognition that he has been conducting a sort of family embezzlement. In hard terms there is less money available and *debts accumulate*. The family has to live at a lower standard. His wife, and understandably so, blames him all the more for this because he corners what money there is and squanders it pointlessly. At the same time she begins to appreciate that they are *becoming isolated socially*. They get less invitations and her husband's state makes her refuse some of those she still receives and would like to accept. Increasingly she has to take over the management of the family and assume the role of the head of the house. It is now the wife who organizes, controls, provides for everybody. She is increasingly driven to brood over the fact that her husband has become inconsiderate, furtive and deceitful, seemingly callous and unfeeling. Added to which, he is often drunk. His manner becomes coarser. He is *repeatedly aggressive*, ill-treating her and abusing the children. At times he may hit. The result of this behaviour is a growing animosity towards him.

As his wife accuses, rails, threatens and humiliates him he retaliates with greater hostility. The alcoholic is unable to see that all these adverse circumstances flow from his drinking. 'At first I compromised between marriage and drink. Then my home began to mean less. I spent increasing time in pubs and wanted more opportunities for drinking.' He is led to *re-interpret events in a paranoid way*. He sees himself as the victim, not as the originator, of the bad things that happen. It is his friends, his employer, his family who have let *him* down. Self-pity has come to partner his remorse.

This is also a point of no return. The opportunity for an important step in insight has been lost. Once he believes himself wronged he ceases to construe the world correctly. He suspects those who try to help him, imagining them imbued with the hostility he senses all about him. Now, when he comes home late he gives himself a new reason for this; his lingering in the pubs was to prepare himself to meet his wife's reproach. Similar *excuses and alibis* justify the opportunities he finds for drinking and his growing inability to meet his responsibilities.

In fact, rationalizations began a long time ago, when he first told himself that a drink with a customer would help him in the way of business. At first, he was persuading himself; now he is persuaded, and it is a short step to being actually deluded. So, for instance, although it is his *diminished sexual drive* which has made intercourse a rare occurrence, he comes to believe that this is the result of his wife's not wanting it. Her coldness provides him with the grain of truth needed to reinforce this notion. Then, suddenly, the idea will come to him that the reason for her unresponsiveness is that she has a lover. He is impervious to reassurance, to protestation; despite all evidence to the contrary he is convinced of her infidelity. He has become *morbidly jealous*.

I picture occasions my wife may have for intercourse. I become

bitter, sick to my stomach, as if it's a lump of lead there. I feel I
must do something more positive. I suspect the paternity of my
second son. Then I wonder over the fact that the daughter coming
after him also has red hair. I ask my wife would she permit a blood
test. I feel low when I am accusing my wife but I have to see if I
can break her down.

Round about this time he may begin to be *continuously drunk
throughout whole weekends*. Friday night to Sunday passes in a
besotted blur. When he returns to sobriety he may be able to
remember very little of how the time has been passed. For the
family, too, it has been a nightmare. If he was in the house and
incapable, he excited their contempt; worse, if he did not come
home, they had to reconcile their anger with their anxiety.

This state is not compatible with his working properly at
the beginning of the week. Missed days of work become more
frequent and eventually he *loses his job*. Either he gets the sack
or, realizing that this is inescapable, he quits. It is more difficult
to find a second job than to keep the first one. His new employer
will feel no compunction at dismissing him. And so it goes on.
He will be forced into increasingly unskilled jobs for less and
less money. He will find himself applying for posts he would
not have considered previously; often he fails to get them.

The family may now break up. He may leave home and go to
live in lodgings where he must fend for himself. In this isolated
state he is suddenly presented with the everyday problem of
keeping his clothes clean and in good repair. He begins to look
seedy and shabby, and this leads him to avoid people more.
The last remnants of self-respect make him shun his friends and
they keep out of his way.

When he wakes up *in the morning he is restless* and anxious and
he finds his hands are shaking. He cannot tie his shoelaces; he
is not able to shave. He discovers that if he takes a drink the
shakes come under control and he is able to complete his
dressing. *Morning drinking* now becomes a regular feature.
Alcohol replaces a more orthodox breakfast for which he has

no stomach. He guards himself from the extremity of being unable to moderate these symptoms by seeing to it that there are *always supplies of drink available*, if necessary by concealing bottles in every possible hiding-place. Sometimes he forgets where he has put them and is beset with terror until he can remember.

A solicitor, still living with his wife, wrote this wry description:

The lavatory cistern's no use – it was in *Whisky Galore*. Behind the pedestal of the wash hand basin in the bathroom is almost a common denominator. The high shelf in the linen cupboard is good enough because you are tall and the wife short. The rabbit hutch is un-doubtedly in the clever class – rabbits can't talk but too sudden an interest in animal life can give rise to disaster. The best of all is undoubtedly the car – that blanked-off bit in the dashboard where the radio used to be, underneath the tool kit, alongside the spare wheel, or just simply in the glove locker with last week's *Sunday Times* on top of it. The decoy system has its merits, involving con-cealment in a place likely to give the hunter sufficient satisfaction in finding it that she will not want to look elsewhere. Perhaps the safest place of all is the inside jacket pocket, provided the tell-tale 'glug, glug' can be eliminated. Ability to remove and replace corks, stoppers, patent tops and the like quickly is another essential for the regular operator and demands constant practice and attention to detail. Nothing is more difficult to hide behind a screen of idle chatter than the all-pervading smell of whisky emanating from a leaking bottle.

He makes attempts to stop because he realizes that drink is conquering him; he may at last be ready to concede that he is an alcoholic and that unless he takes himself in hand he is lost. With a mixture of determination and hopelessness he may actually abstain for as long as a few weeks, though generally these *dry periods* are measured in days only. Each spell is pain-fully achieved for to begin it he must endure the physical and mental agony of withdrawal symptoms. One patient said:

I realized I was drinking too much and for about a year I managed to cut my input down; I restricted my drinking to weekends and drank mostly beer. But I gradually slipped back into the old pattern. Occasionally I tried to stop altogether but couldn't.

Sometimes there is an unfortunate accompaniment of these attempts to give up drinking. The alcoholic may seek to relieve the tension he feels by *recourse to drugs* – generally either barbiturate sleeping tablets or stimulants of the benzedrine group. The habit of taking these drugs is then likely to persist and is an additional serious complication.

After each attempt to stop, drinking starts up again and with it there is mounting dejection. *Suicide attempts* are frequent, episodes of self-poisoning or self-injury which the alcoholic survives.

I was dry for almost a month but at my cousin's wedding I felt different from the others. I decided to have one drink. I thought I could control it. The old alcoholic delusion. . . . I drank without restraint for the next five days. In a blinding flash of drunken logic I saw how bad I was. It was a shattering thunderbolt. I took a handful of pills, not as a cry for help but because of the hopeless position I was in.

Such suicide attempts generally take place during a drinking spell, and the disturbance in thinking caused by intoxication distorts both the motive and the planning. Very often an overdose of pills is taken impulsively, without more than a moment's consideration. When such patients recover consciousness in hospital they often cannot explain why they did it. Those who can may be unsure whether they intended to die or to force their plight upon people's notice. A man woke one morning to find himself sitting in his car in a park. He had had an amnesia. He had no idea how he got there. In a panic he drove to his home. His wife had left, taking all her belongings. He drank more, wrote a farewell letter to his wife and got into his car. 'I decided to crash in my car.' He drove at great speed into a lorry. He was taken to hospital unconscious with a fractured skull.

Underlying all these attempts is *despair*, sometimes arising suddenly after an evening's drinking, sometimes brooded over at length. Almost every alcoholic who has reached this degree of illness has ruminated that he would be better out of the way, better dead. Many, in fact, kill themselves.

CHRONIC ALCOHOLISM

He is not eating enough; he cannot be bothered to cook and the prolonged effect of alcohol on the stomach has taken his appetite away. He is almost continuously nauseated. *Neglect of nutrition* may lead to physical illness and this may give the doctor his first opportunity to discover the facts and confront the alcoholic with the diagnosis. Nutritional disorders develop. He has clear-cut physical disease. He is a chronic alcoholic.

He *steeps himself in drink*. The uninterrupted binges of intoxication, the prolonged periods of continuous drunkenness, may be produced by less and less alcohol, for the body's *tolerance diminishes* quite sharply at this time. The alcoholic discovers that he cannot drink anything like the quantity that he formerly consumed. His reduced intake no longer satisfies and, what is more, it makes him disorganized and helpless whereas previously he had prided himself on how much he could take without getting drunk. Alcoholics always realize that this reduction in tolerance indicates a serious physical deterioration. Although his binges are no longer pleasurable he has to give himself up to them. He must have drink and to get it he will go to any lengths. He may start *drinking cheap wines*, even methylated spirits.

He becomes the *victim of terrifying fears*. Sometimes these accompany his drinking. Most of the time his *thinking is confused*. He only knows that not to drink is torture but drinking itself no longer brings relief. He may now seek the help of

Alcoholics Anonymous or go to a doctor for medical advice about alcoholism. He may get this, however, only when he is admitted to hospital with a *serious illness*, either a physical condition, usually cirrhosis of the liver or peripheral neuritis, or else with a psychiatric complication, delirium tremens, alcoholic epilepsy or a psychosis.

To continue drinking is now impossible; yet to stop is unthinkable. He admits total defeat. His only way out is to find treatment.

Chapter 9

THE ALCOHOLIC'S FAMILY

ALCOHOLICS, as we have seen, conform to definite types both in personality and in drinking pattern. Similarly there are recognized patterns of behaviour in their wives. Partly these are evolved as responses to the husband's drinking, but we ought to consider whether they might not have been present in the wife earlier. Do alcoholics, in fact, select certain types of women and are there women who are particularly attracted to alcoholics? We must remember that at the time of the marriage alcoholism or even excessive drinking may not have developed. The man when he marries may have only the predisposition to alcoholism and the woman who accepts him may be choosing a husband because his personality characteristics appeal to her.

The wife of an alcoholic, much more frequently than chance would account for, is the daughter of an alcoholic. She may be seeking to revive in her marriage the relationship which she had with her father. Because she can see the justness of her friends' warnings she may be hard put to it to account for her persistence in wanting to marry the man of her choice. She may marry him sensing full well that the marriage is not going to be happy. Her parents' objections are also no deterrent.

Alcoholics frequently marry women older than themselves. This has been documented by Duchene[1], though not found by Åmark.[2] It may perhaps indicate that the husband seeks maternal responses from his wife; he has created a psychological

1. Duchène, H., Schutzenberger, M. P., Biro, J. and Schmitz, B. (1952). 'Ages of couples where the husband is alcoholic'. *La Semaine des Hôpitaux de Paris, 28*, 1857.

2. Åmark, C. (1951). 'A study in alcoholism'. *Acta Psychologica et Neurologica Scandinavica*, Supplement 70.

equivalent of his relationship with his mother. Some men who marry older women are sexually inhibited. They may tolerate, even welcome, being dominated by their wives who are the real authorities in the family. In the case of an alcoholic this domination is frequently benign. His wife may enjoy mothering her husband, even when she has young children to nurture. She loves babies, wants many of them and may happily number her husband among them. Apart from isolated observations like these, our information about wives of alcoholics is derived from questioning them after the alcoholism has developed. An alcoholic's wife often admits that she was aware that her husband drank a lot at the time she married him, but she will claim that she had not realized the implications of this. She expresses surprise, in retrospect, that she failed to do so. Many women, on the other hand, marry excessive drinkers believing that they will have a reforming influence upon their husbands. They do not realize how beset with conflict the marriage will be. From the wife's standpoint, her husband will not be dependable; she will have to manage the greater part of the household responsibilities on her own; she cannot rely on him to play his part either in making important decisions, for instance about the children's education, or in simple day-to-day choices such as planning leisure activities. Very often she will have to go out to work and there may be periods during which he is unemployed and she is the bread-winner. What assistance he renders then takes the form of domestic duties, cooking, cleaning and childminding.

She becomes insensitive to the effect on him of her constantly disparaging and belittling reaction. One wife, genuinely anxious to be helpful to her husband, described in detail his 'dim-witted behaviour'. She dwelt with careful emphasis on his social clumsiness.

He tries desperately hard. He wants to be extra nice. He says unusual things, like 'What a nice hat' – you know – without realizing sufficiently that what he is saying is unusual. When there is talk about business, he makes remarks which have an air of wisdom but nothing behind them. When people ask him a question about his work or something factual the answer he gives is perfectly futile, even to an outsider. I feel that anyone would know it was a guess. In conversation with me, and particularly when we have other people around, he will make statements about matters of which he knows nothing. They are totally incorrect, and he can't substantiate them. He tries to, if discussion arises, not really aggressively but . . . he feels he has to assert himself. He makes the mistake of thinking that what matters is asserting himself and not being sure if he is right when he does so.

More than one writer has stressed how capable the alcoholic's wife is. She can generally manage the household affairs on her own and, to the outsider at least, she seems to have no great need for an adequate husband. Towards her children she feels competent to combine the father's role with her own. And by assuming this complete parental function she diminishes her husband in his own eyes, underlining his sense of inadequacy.

This view of the wife as a determining or at least an aggravating factor in her husband's alcoholism comes readily to psychiatrists and social workers whose focus of concern must be with the patient. Because they must mobilize every resource towards improving his condition they are apt to concentrate on those facets of the wife's behaviour which may be exacerbating his drinking. Some wives feel, when their husbands are receiving treatment, that the psychiatrist is inferring that they are somehow to blame for their husband's condition. If this suggestion is indeed made to them too directly they are naturally disturbed. If either party merits criticism, the wife considers it is surely the offending husband for the way he has treated her.

The alcoholic makes things very hard for his wife. At the most material level, she is denied the necessary money to manage the house and she knows where it is going. When she protests, he may make promises but matters always get worse.

How could they improve if he is compelled to spend upwards of seven pounds a week on drink? It costs more than that for half a bottle of whisky a day if you drink at home. In pubs it is more. Try as she may, the wife cannot maintain the home standards she wishes and feels that she justly deserves. Debts mount but her husband appears unconcerned. It is she who meets the tradesman at the door, and when she plans to economize she gets no support from her husband.

Socially too he is no longer dependable. She never knows when he will be home for meals, and if she prepares food it may be wasted. She cannot arrange for them to go out to friends for he may not be willing. She dare not invite friends home for he may not be sober. In short she cannot plan, so no coherent way of life is possible for her. Alcoholics' wives wait. They wait for their husbands to come home; they wait for an accident; they wait for their husbands to lose their jobs. They wait for the inevitable catastrophe.

The alcoholic's wife witnesses his intoxicated behaviour, day after day, week after week, with increasing abhorrence. He himself is only partly aware of what he is doing. It is she who sees how appalling some of his actions are. His cigarettes burn holes in the carpet and the bedding. At times he seems blatantly loutish and brutish to her. Mostly she feels that he is incapable of decent behaviour. His behaviour always hurts whether she regards this as intentional on his part or not. She sees him insidiously and progressively destroying all she had come to hope for and expect from life. She may have to endure his violence; by no means all alcoholics are violent when intoxicated, but many knock their wives about. He may be jealous and accuse her of going with other men. She can be severely ill-treated, both physically and mentally.

His sexual approaches may repel her by their unfeeling clumsiness. What has been of emotional importance is now only sordid and loathsome. Fear of becoming pregnant when her husband is in such a state increases her distaste for intercourse, which seems to her to be degrading, merely a satisfying of his transient and ineffective lust.

She misses the companionship, the warmth and understanding which a husband should provide. There is no opportunity for them to talk together, so she cannot convey to him her own thoughts and experiences and needs. Even were she able to, she questions whether he would understand, appreciate and respond. She feels herself increasingly solitary, her life arid from the lack of affection and the impossibility of expressing tenderness towards him.

A wife may lavish this uninvested emotion on the children, swamping them with excessive demands to make good the deficit in her marriage and to provide the affection which she does not get from her husband. Children are not mature enough to meet these emotional pressures and their own development can be harmed by the pressures upon them to do so.

The alcoholic's wife is bewildered. She is unable to put into perspective what has happened in her life. She ponders whether she has brought it upon herself. She fears at times that she may be responsible for her husband's drinking. She cannot decide if he is unfeeling, wilful or sick. She does not know if it is more appropriate for her to be angry or protective. She does not know what view to take of the problem or to whom to turn for help. She may continue for a long time, vainly hoping that her husband is just going through a bad patch, that the upset is only temporary, and that by his own efforts he will yet manage to control his drinking.

She spends a lot of her energy covering up for him. She dissembles to his employers about his lateness, his absences or his early departures from work. She parries neighbours' puzzled inquiries or unwanted expressions of sympathy. She attempts, with less success than she knows, to conceal from her children the slights to which she is subjected and the quarrels which ensue. Her parents begin urging her to take a strong line with him, even to leave him, and she is in conflict between

her filial and her wifely loyalties. Even if she feels whole-
heartedly that she ought to take her husband's side, she knows
that she may later have to depend on her parents should the
situation worsen.

The wife tries what have been called 'home remedies',[1] the
vain devices aimed at removing available liquor. Bottles are
searched for, emptied down the sink, hidden; attempts are
made to control the money, to persuade shops not to allow
credit. Decisions are made, promises extracted, ultimatums
delivered. The wife persists in the hopeless sequence of plead-
ing, argument, hostility, hatred because she does not grasp yet
that, much as her husband would wish to stop drinking, only
with specialized outside assistance will he be able to give up
alcohol. In the meantime, the family may live through quarrels,
terror, physical assault and neighbourhood disgrace. The wife
may be unable to tolerate more distress, or she may decide that
for the sake of the children she has to leave her husband.

If she can only come to understand that what besets her
husband is illness, a new way of dealing with her total problem
opens to her. She can cease to hold her husband responsible for
what he is doing to her and her natural affection and sympathies
for him need no longer be withheld. She is not out of the wood
by this realization.

A patient's wife was telling the doctor about his behaviour
when drinking, alternately talking to the doctor and rounding
on her husband who was present:

Once he starts drinking nothing you say makes sense to him.
There's an imbecilic look on his face. You're just not in the same
world at all. It's a completely different person! He talks rubbish.
Everything makes him quarrelsome. You get the failings of everybody thrown at you all the time. I don't think you even remember
what happens, or all the things you say. An objectionable, horrible
person, *completely* different. Such a horrible creature. It's a terrible

1. Mann, M. (1950). *Primer on Alcoholism*. New York: Rinehart & Co.,
Inc.

Jekyll and Hyde thing. It's as if he takes a blackout or a brainstorm. It's not that he's drunk: all sense seems to go completely out.

It's difficult to move him from one room to another. You try to make him go into the bedroom, to get him out of sight. He fights you. You try to stop him from damaging himself when swaying too violently. You can't reason with him – I'm told I'm completely useless, quite hopeless, I'm told I can't face life as it really is. I find bottles about the room and tell him. He says, 'There were no bottles in the room.' He tells me he has stopped, and I find one bottle in the bed and one under the car seat. Then he drinks champagne to celebrate finishing with drink for all time. You really have to live with it to know what it's like. My goodness, I can sympathize with any wife who goes through this. Now I've got to think of the boys – my one son is disgusted with his father; the other won't go near him.

When the wife stopped speaking her husband glared at her and said quietly: 'What you really want to see happen is that I should be locked up.' His wife did not deny the hostility she had been driven to feel. She said helplessly, 'If I stopped seeing it as an illness that would be hopeless. If I thought he could help it, that would be the end.'

The wife who has learnt to regard her husband's alcoholism as an illness can go on to orient her own life with greater assurance even should her husband continue to drink. As far as her feelings are concerned she may still oscillate between sympathy and anger. But she no longer has to feel ineffectual, overwhelmed by the problem. She can now approach the resources in society that can provide help. Professional people are becoming increasingly enlightened about the problem of alcoholism, and the misguided attitudes of previous times are giving way to better counsels today. So the doctor, the minister, the lawyer, the social worker need not nowadays limit their advice to moralizing. The doctor can advise a suitable course of action and inform the wife what treatment will be available. She may be recommended to adopt a certain approach if her husband is cooperative, but if he is not she can still be helped to

decide what to do. There are few doctors today who will tell
the wife that her alcoholic husband is worthless, urging her to
leave him. Ministers can offer practical advice to suit the particular need in addition to the prayer and faith which they have
always advocated. Social workers no longer dispense ready-
made drastic advice or solutions, but investigate with the wife
the special circumstances of her case. Should she want to stay
with her husband, this will be appreciated by members of these
helping professions. If she is determined to leave him, they will
not criticize. If she cannot make up her mind they will not make
the decision for her but will assist her in weighing up the merits
of each course. A decision on her part to separate may not be
the drastic undoing of her husband that she fears. The fact of a
wife's leaving may make an alcoholic more prepared to go for
treatment. An excess of care by a supportive wife, especially if
the dependent relationship shields the alcoholic from what
would otherwise be the realities of his addiction, may actually
militate against his acceptance of medical treatment.

Marriages of alcoholics are often interrupted by separations
and many end in divorce. Either the alcoholic or the spouse
may initiate the separation but it is usually the latter because the
alcoholic has much more to lose than to gain by leaving home.
If we are considering male alcoholics it is generally late in the
progress of the condition that they quit the home and often
it is the wife who brings this about, not the alcoholic. Sometimes the wife leaves, taking the children with her and retreating
to her mother's house or to another member of the family. She
does it because she can no longer stick the drunken behaviour
at home and the humiliation of never being able to go out or to
have friends call; she does it to protect her children from the
repugnant sight of their father and, last but not least, she does
it to exert pressure on him to stop drinking or to go for treatment. These separations may not last long; the wife yields to his
pleas for her return and his protestations that he will reform.
When next he relapses it will be less of a struggle for her to

leave. So there are often a number of separations. By themselves these do not necessarily indicate that the marriage will end. It is considerably more likely to do so when the husband has lost his job or has been physically violent to his family. Then his wife often concludes that the marriage is hopeless and makes a decision never to return. Whether or not such a final separation is taken to the divorce courts depends on many extraneous factors.

It is much less common for a wife to leave an alcoholic husband than for a husband to leave an alcoholic wife. Women alcoholics have less stable marriages than do male alcoholics. Fox[1] suggests three reasons for this: that drinking by men is more socially acceptable, that women have mothering impulses which they can extend to their drinking husbands, and that in harsh economic terms wives are financially dependent on husbands. To these we would add a fourth: women alcoholic patients have in the main more disturbed personalities than their male counterparts.

When the wife remains with her husband she may none the less harbour intensely painful feelings of resentment and anger towards him. She is sometimes not fully aware of this hostility. Though she does not voice it directly she can use others in the family to give expression to it.

An alcoholic gave up drink when treated, and after leaving hospital returned to work and regularly attended the weekly out-patient psychotherapeutic group in which he was exploring his inter-personal problems.

His wife's father, who lived in the house with them, was an irritation to the patient. The old man would rarely leave the house: he was involved in all the family discussions, recalling how difficult the alcoholic had been, the hardships his daughter had suffered, the disadvantages inflicted on the children, and so on. When the patient had a temporary lapse he was ashamed

1. Fox, R. (1956). 'The alcoholic spouse'. In *Neurotic Interaction in Marriage*, ed. Eisenstein, V. W. New York: Basic Books, Inc.

and dejected. To his wife's reproaches were added the old man's portentous predictions of imminent disaster: everything was hopeless, all was now lost. The alcoholic drank more, grabbed sleeping pills from the medicine cupboard and swallowed a large number in the presence of his wife and father-in-law. He sat down and gradually got drowsy. As he became unconscious, the father urged: 'Leave him'. It was only when the 12-year-old son returned home that the mother was persuaded to call the doctor, who then summoned an ambulance to convey the by now unconscious man to hospital.

There are marriages in which the wife of the alcoholic herself becomes ill. Sometimes this happens when the husband stops drinking, the first symptoms appearing when he assumes increasing family responsibility. When this occurs it is a serious added strain to the husband, often jeopardizing his recovery. Fortunately it is not common.

Another alcoholic had recovered satisfactorily with treatment and resumed his part in his family's affairs. An unmarried daughter had become pregnant, and when the time came for her delivery she was living in a distant city with a married sister. The recovered patient wanted to go with his wife on the visit she had planned to support her daughter through this difficult time. He intended to urge his daughter to end her association with the man responsible for the pregnancy.

He succeeded in conveying his point of view, but his wife became involved in a quarrel with the married daughter whose house it was. As a result, she was told to leave. Thereupon she lost her memory, and for months afterwards was disabled by a psychological disorder of fluctuating severity, in which she was unable to recall how many children she had, and how old they were; at times she was even uncertain whether she was married or not.

Notwithstanding the great stresses imposed, a great number of wives stay with their husbands through painful years of disappointment, debt and humiliation; they assist them energetically to obtain treatment, seek advice themselves to understand how they might have contributed to their husbands' difficulty, and are profoundly happy with the contentment and order which results when their husbands' drinking stops.

CHILDREN OF ALCOHOLICS

A competent mother can make up for most of the deficiencies resulting from a father's alcoholism. So pronounced are the capabilities of alcoholics' wives to sustain the roles proper to their husbands that the children do not commonly suffer material privation. Myers[1] found that the children of a series of London alcoholics rarely went hungry and were always well cared for. Inevitably the personal development of the children of an alcoholic must be anomalous; for one thing there are likely to be unwanted changes of home with consequent disruptions of schooling and of friendships. But this need not give rise to any adult abnormality. They are certain to have a decided attitude towards drinkers and drinking. Either they tend to drink excessively themselves or they are strongly opposed to it. Sons of alcoholics frequently become alcoholic themselves. Their personalities have been labelled[2] 'passive-aggressive'; they often have serious difficulty in expressing assertive impulses and in knowing what to do with angry feelings aroused by frustrating situations. Alcoholics often stress that they have perceived their drinking fathers as nebulous family members, inaccessible when their presence was longed for. These sons envied other boys who were proud of fathers that took an interest in their achievements and played with them.

The alcoholic father is often as good as absent, always liable to erupt unpredictably with some behaviour which embarrasses

1. Myers, E. (1954). 'Alcoholics and their families'. *Case Conference, 1,* 4.
2. Aronson, H. and Gilbert, A. (1963). 'Pre-adolescent sons of male alcoholics'. *Archives of General Psychiatry, 8,* 235.

or wounds the family. The children quickly pick up cues from their mother, leading them to look down on their father and condemn his standards and actions. A son of such a father never loses the impact made on him by the paternal failure. One alcoholic would never enter a hotel; he could not bring himself to do so, being constrained by recollections of repeated humiliations during his adolescence caused by his father's uncouth and uninhibited behaviour to waitresses. He felt himself enfeebled and deprived through never having had a father who could be respected.

The effect of an alcoholic parent persists throughout life; its influence is subtle and strong. Attitudes are conditioned by it, whether or not the individual is aware of this. We have seen that a girl whose father was an alcoholic will often marry a passive man, perhaps even an alcoholic himself. She may repeat the same pattern two or three times. An alcoholic father provides an unserviceable personality model.

In Sweden children of alcoholic fathers were compared with similar children from non-alcoholic families.[1] The ages ranged from 4 to 12 years. (Divorce or separation had taken place in 28 per cent of the alcoholic families and in 4 per cent of the control families.) One of the comparisons made was in attendances at hospital. Twenty-four per cent from the alcoholics' families, and a similar figure, 19 per cent, from the controls' had been to hospital. But whereas two thirds of the control children had organic causes found to account for their physical symptoms, this was true for only a quarter of the alcoholics' children. Three quarters of them were not considered to have an organic basis to explain their complaints. Attendances at child guidance clinics, for psychiatric disorder, were the same for the two groups of children. When their teachers were questioned they rated 48 per cent of children from alcoholic families as problem children, but only 10 per cent of those from non-alcoholic homes.

1. Nylander, I. (1960). *See p. 71.*

Tension in the child shows not only in the form of illnesses and abnormal behaviour at school but also by disturbed relationships at home. Where the father is alcoholic an intensified relationship is set up between the children and their mother; she may thus unwittingly become the recipient of hostile and resentful feelings which the total family situation has engendered in the children. In carrying out the breadwinning role, the mother has perforce to neglect some of her other functions. Nylander found that the alcoholics' children who had had to be admitted to hospital for psychiatric care seemed to have more problems concerning their mothers than their fathers.

The effect upon the child of an alcoholic parent is considerably reduced if the other parent is able to provide a sympathetic explanation of the condition in terms of illness. This enables the child to understand why the father fails so grossly in his paternal role, and so spares the growing child some of the harmful effects which result when a father is viewed with contempt.

Chapter 10

TREATMENT

TREATMENT of an alcoholic is a large endeavour and the programme for any particular patient has to be designed to suit his individual needs. We can, however, distinguish separate phases.

The first phase is acceptance of the need for treatment. It is hard for non-alcoholics to realize what a surrender of pride is involved. The alcoholic has to appreciate that he is an alcoholic and that he must stop drinking. This may not be too difficult. His life circumstances will force the knowledge on him and as we have already seen he has probably made one or more unsuccessful attempts to give up on his own. The next step follows from this and is far harder for him to adopt. He needs to accept that he cannot become abstinent without help. Despite the evidence to the contrary provided by repeated failures in the past, alcoholics often insist that they can overcome their addiction on their own. Physicians in general hospitals who deal with the medical crises of alcoholism are constantly being told: 'This time I'm *determined* to give it up. I can do it myself. This time I know I'll give it up.'

Spontaneous cures of alcoholism are reported. In many of them religious conversion plays a part. However, they are so rare that the National Council on Alcoholism advises: 'It can be done but the odds are against trying.'

Before any treatment can be effective this attitude has to be altered; for the doctor it may be a painstaking task to help his patient overcome it. Partly it is based on the fear of having to give up drinking that is mixed with his desire to do so. Although he sees how it has ruined his life the alcoholic at the same time knows that, so far, alcohol has been the only solution he has found for his problems. He is not ready to give it up until he is sure that there is another course open to him.

The second phase, which may or may not be necessary, consists of general medical treatment of the physical diseases wrought by alcoholism. Alcoholic gastritis subsides spontaneously when drinking is given up and with it goes much of the nausea and lack of appetite of which the alcoholic complains. Indeed the loss of these symptoms is often the first benefit noted by the newly abstinent alcoholic. Cirrhosis of the liver requires a much more complicated régime of management. The nutritional disorders and the vitamin deficiency diseases are dealt with by restoring an adequate diet and by giving vitamin supplements, in particular one constituent of the B complex, thiamine. The disorders of the nervous system, if they are not too advanced, respond to this therapy but they do so very slowly and in some cases without full restitution to normal.

Withdrawal symptoms may also need active physical measures for their treatment or prevention.

Withdrawal symptoms can fortunately be averted or abated without the necessity of giving more alcohol (though in the past this means of treatment was used). Nowadays one of the tranquillizing drugs is given, generally chlorpromazine (largactil). It is prescribed to prevent the development of withdrawal symptoms when these can be anticipated, and to modify and abate them when they occur. This drug, when it is administered in adequate dosage, makes the full-blown picture of florid delirium tremens now not nearly as common as it used to be; and if the condition has developed it is capable of terminating it within a few hours.

Our principal concern in this chapter is the management of alcohol addiction. An alcoholic can embark on this phase when he has accepted the need for treatment and when the necessary medical measures have restored his physical health. He is asking for help, he is ready for it and this is the time when he should get it. He is often advised to enter hospital at the beginning of his anti-addictive treatment. There are many reasons for this but the most important is that in hospital he is removed from alcohol. Until he is sober, until his thinking processes are back to normal, there can be no adequate communication between the doctor and the patient. The doctor cannot learn the significant details of his particular problems, and the patient cannot command the foresight necessary to examine his own situation and to respond to the physician's approach. After some weeks (the time varies with the patient's rate of progress and the physician's practice) he leaves hospital to continue active treatment as an out-patient.

The techniques of treatment that are used during both in-patient and out-patient periods are various, being designed to protect the patient from lapsing into renewed drinking, to enable him to appreciate the reasons for his dependence on alcohol and hence to overcome them and to foster his resources for coping better socially.

The alcoholic who is going to give up drinking will inevitably have to depend on and trust somebody whom he accepts as prepared to help him and has the necessary skills. If he decides on medical treatment there are a number of approaches he can make. In the first instance he may attend his general practitioner.

THE GENERAL PRACTITIONER

The alcoholic who goes to his general practitioner and asks specifically for treatment can pose his doctor with a demand which neither his medical-school training nor his professional experience has equipped him to meet. The doctor's response, therefore, may be to indicate that this is not a matter for him, or he may selectively attend to the physical aspects of the disorder, or he may refer the patient to a specialist. Many patients report that their general practitioners do not seem to have taken their alcoholism seriously.

If the general practitioner also attends the wife, the patient may feel, sometimes correctly, that the doctor is more concerned with her point of view than his own. The patient will be dismayed if the doctor seems to hold him responsible for the wife's unhappiness, especially if his strictures are accompanied by ineffectual advice to give it up. 'Just do your best', a general practitioner had urged an alcoholic we heard speak at an AA meeting. When they refer patients to specialist care few practitioners seem to do so with an air of confidence in the outcome, thereby conveying to the patient that he was right to come to the doctor and is now being sent to get the treatment that will help him recover. The alcoholic is more likely to get the impression that the doctor is passing him on and is not prepared to maintain a continuing interest.

If the general practitioner does not appreciate the problem of alcoholism this is because of lack of knowledge about the nature and treatment of the disorder. The subject is likely to have been ignored in his medical-student training unless he qualified fairly recently, and opportunities for postgraduate instruction are meagre. Not all teachers are persuaded that the subject merits emphasis; some are opposed to any teaching about alcoholism being given in a general-practitioner postgraduate psychiatry course. Yet a joint committee of the Medical Association and the Magistrates' Association[1] stressed that the problem in Britain was 'of the size to merit urgent attention'. They stated clearly that few doctors have a training which enables them to manage a case of alcoholism and pointed out that neither general nor psychiatric hospitals do much to meet the special needs of the alcoholic. The committee urged more training for doctors in the recognition and treatment of alcoholism.

In the meantime, until there is wider professional under-

1. *British Medical Journal Supplement*, 1961, *1*, 190.

standing about alcoholism, the alcoholic needs to ascertain for himself whether his family doctor will approach his problem with understanding and sympathy.

We consider that, ideally, general practitioners should possess sufficient knowledge of the illness of alcoholism to understand that patients cannot recover by their own efforts. Therefore they should know what treatment facilities are available in their own area and if necessary be prepared to press for better ones. They should take an active part in the after-care of patients who have received specialist treatment. What they know about the patient and his family could be of the greatest value. Above all, the single contribution which they could most easily make to the problem of alcoholism is to respond to all the vicissitudes of an alcoholic's illness with the same calm professional concern that they show towards other illnesses.

THE GENERAL HOSPITAL PHYSICIAN

The general hospital has a crucial part to play in the management of alcoholics. Its functions should include the alleviation of withdrawal symptoms and the treatment of the medical complications of alcoholism. General physicians must also be vigilant to recognize alcoholism in their patients and should take responsibility for seeing that such patients are referred for treatment of their addiction. The advent of the tranquillizing drugs like chlorpromazine has made possible the treatment of withdrawal symptoms in general medical wards. Agitation can now be controlled, so that restless patients need not disturb other patients. Hospital policy in many cases lags behind this therapeutic advance, so that although a physician wishes to admit an alcoholic to his beds for this necessary purpose he may encounter resistance from colleagues and from the nursing and administrative staff. Yet there is nowhere better than the general ward in which to detect somatic illnesses resulting from alcoholism. The effects of interference with nutrition can be corrected by the administration of large amounts of vitamins by injection. With such responsible medical care many alcoholics will be substantially helped to begin their recovery.

Hospital staff are all too unaware how important it is to alcoholics that they be accepted in hospitals as rightful patients, entitled to professional care for the tremulousness, body aches, restlessness and anxiety, perhaps seizures and even delirious states which may manifest as alcohol leaves the body. For many alcoholics it would be unthinkable to weather this transition phase between drinking and abstinence without such care. The patient who receives such management is on the threshold of abstinence. His prospects suddenly look very different. He is now able to think rationally and to take stock of his situation with his mind unimpaired by the chronic toxic effects of alcohol.

THE PSYCHIATRIST

The psychiatrist should be called in as soon as the patient is admitted to the general hospital. Indeed, he may often have seen the patient already and arranged the admission. During the period of physical treatment he will be establishing a relationship with the patient, which will continue after the need for treatment in the general ward is over and the primary responsibility for the patient's care passes to him.

The patient will be transferred to a psychiatric unit, which may be a ward in the general hospital, or a psychiatric hospital, or may be a specialized unit for alcoholism situated in either.

There are 4,000 alcoholics admitted annually to psychiatric hospitals in Britain. They go into over 150 such hospitals. Unfortunately, most of these hospitals have no special programme in operation for treating alcoholics. Only in a handful are there psychiatrists who are especially interested and experienced. Unless a treatment programme is provided for them alcoholic patients may receive little attention during their stay in hospital and their willingness to persist in treatment will accordingly be lost. Under such conditions they will almost certainly not be prevented from drinking again when they are discharged. Many alcoholics recount the dismal charade that goes on of bottles of whisky being smuggled into the hospital for covert consumption by despairing patients. The time passed by the alcoholic in such hospitals may allow him to recoup his physical strength but otherwise it is wastefully spent. When the patient is discharged he and his doctor may part company, sometimes with mutual relief; neither feels he has succeeded. The lack of planned treatment in hospital is frequently matched by a failure to provide adequate outpatient care after discharge. This unsatisfactory state of affairs does not prevail in every psychiatric hospital. Some are outstandingly active in their treatment programmes for alcoholics.

THE QUESTION OF COMPULSION

Regularly the question of compulsory treatment of alcoholics is aired. This is in spite of evidence that where acceptable services are provided alcoholics use them voluntarily. Few psychiatrists are satisfied by the results achieved when patients are compelled into their care. Patient and doctor regard each other with antipathy and it is not possible to provide more than custodial treatment. But even today their general medical colleagues seem unable to relinquish a groundless belief in the benefits of treatment by compulsion. The way they formulate this indicates that such compulsory detention in hospital also serves a punishing role: 'We feel that in some very bad cases, compulsory detention in hospital offers the only hope of successful treatment.' 'We believe that some alcoholics would welcome compulsory removal and detention in hospital until treatment is completed.'[1]

1. British Medical Association (Scottish Office). *Memorandum of Evidence to the Standing Medical Advisory Committee's Special Sub-committee on Alcoholism*, May 1964.

The same report continues: 'Unfortunately, very few alcoholics really want to be "cured". It is seldom the alcoholic that makes the original approach to his general practitioner for treatment; it is almost always his relatives.' The opinion was given that the majority of alcoholics 'and even potential alcoholics' require hospital in-patient treatment for at least several months. 'For psychological and social reasons, the unit should be as far from the patient's home as possible....'

We have quoted these views not just to show that opinions rendered obsolete by research are still firmly put forward, but to indicate the sort of treatment services that, all too possibly, might be set up if administrative decisions were based on such opinions rather than on ascertained facts.

SPECIAL UNITS FOR THE TREATMENT OF ALCOHOLISM

There is increasing demand for specialized units for the treatment of alcoholism to be set up in Britain. The model for such centres was established by the Yale Plan Clinics, the first of which opened in Connecticut in 1944.[1] The essential of treatment in these clinics was the provision of a team comprising a psychiatrist, a general physician, a psychologist, a social worker and a secretary. If they were to function effectively the clinics had to be situated in the community which they served.

The most valuable asset of a specialized unit is trained and experienced staff who regard alcoholism as an illness and approach alcoholics without hostility or contempt. Nurses soon learn to respond to alcoholics without moralizing or condescension but they still require training and supervision to develop the necessary special clinical skills. Treatment staff who are judgemental, or who are liable to react with censure or

1. McCarthy, R. G. (1946). 'A public clinic approach to certain aspects of alcoholism'. *Quarterly Journal of Studies on Alcoholism*, 6, 500.

disapproval if a patient discloses disturbing material, forfeit the chance of continuing to be useful to that patient.

The specialist clinic provides alcoholics with a treatment facility to which they can go when in need. The staff work as a team and provide a coordinated handling of the medical, psychological and social problems of each patient. The psychiatrist integrates the contributions of each member of the treatment staff and formulates for each patient the treatment approach that will be adopted. The psychiatric social worker, customarily a woman, although men work very well with alcoholics and their wives, is a very necessary member of the therapeutic team. She will not find a job or a home for the alcoholic; nor will she settle his debts; but she can show him where to start, how to break up a seemingly overwhelming burden into smaller, manageable portions. Similarly she can assist the patient and his wife to a better understanding of each other's point of view. Usually she will set about this by seeing the wife on many occasions. When the alcoholic first begins treatment his wife often feels that her difficulties are not appreciated and that the patient's account of the marital relationship is being accepted uncritically, so much so that she is regarded by the doctor as more to blame than her husband. It is the job of the social worker to be concerned with her point of view, to support her in her difficulties and yet to show her dispassionately what is happening to her husband and how she can help him at the present juncture. The psychiatric social worker can act as a non-participant go-between, to point out to both parties how they act in opposition to each other.

The job of the social worker does not end there for, in the period after the abstinent patient leaves hospital, he and his wife will have to learn to readjust to a new situation. He will wish to take over the reins of management again and she perhaps be loath to relinquish them, being with reason unsure whether it is going to last. If for the last few years a wife has conducted the entire financial running of a failing business and the domestic economy, she may not be willing to see this authority depart from her, especially into the hands of a potential squanderer. Yet the patient will have been encouraged by his doctor to accept more responsibility and will feel himself fit to do so. Many remissions achieved in hospital flounder because of failure to reconcile the marriage partners and it is primarily the task of the psychiatric social worker in the therapeutic team to help overcome marital difficulties.

The psychologist helps in the assessment of the patient's abilities and in providing vocational advice.

Patients in a special unit learn from witnessing how their *own* illness manifests in others.

The patients attending such a clinic, a specialized unit, may be of a different type from those generally met with in the wards of a psychiatric hospital. Most of them are employed; they are still living with their wives and taking an active part in the life of the community. This also was the finding of Straus and Bacon, who reported on 2,000 alcoholics treated in community clinics in the United States.[1] They found that the type of men who came for treatment differed greatly from what had been expected and called for a revision in the medical stereotype of the alcoholic. These patients were by no means deteriorated socially but had a high degree of social and occupational integration in the community. They came spontaneously to clinics situated near their homes, which provided treatment facilities allowing them to keep up their work and family ties.

The Ministry of Health recommended in a memorandum issued to hospital authorities in 1962 that special units for alcoholics should be established. Hospital boards were urged to establish one unit in each of the twenty hospital regions in Great Britain and increase this provision if necessary. The need for such units to maintain out-patient clinics as well was stressed. To site such clinics far from patients' homes is unreal-

1. Straus, R. and Bacon, S. D. (1951). 'Alcoholism and social stability'. *Quarterly Journal of Studies on Alcohol, 12,* 231.

istic on a number of counts. The alcoholic patient's motivation is his greatest treatment asset; he should be able to find an immediate and convenient response when he makes his initial appeal for help. He should resume his community ties as swiftly as possible. His in-patient and out-patient stages of treatment should be provided by the same service, which cannot be done if the in-patient unit is far from his home. His wife needs to be seen repeatedly to help her gain the understanding of the illness needed if she is to help her husband during his recovery.

What are the forms of treatment which a patient can expect to receive in a special unit for the treatment of alcoholism? We shall first outline the methods which we advocate. Individual patients require individual treatment plans but on the whole this is the customary approach.

It involves: the use of drugs to make it easier for the patient to abstain, the commonest used being antabuse; individual or group therapy; and, where it is considered appropriate, the assistance of Alcoholics Anonymous.

Treatment generally begins with the patient in hospital and continues on an out-patient basis.

Although the most important element in the treatment programme is psychotherapy, we begin by discussing antabuse, because it is introduced at the onset of the treatment programme.

ANTABUSE

Antabuse is the well-known trade name for the chemical compound disulfiram. It comes in tablet form. By itself it produces no effects. However, it interferes with the way the body deals with alcohol. When alcohol is metabolized in the body it is oxidized to carbon dioxide and water. At an intermediate stage in this chemical process a toxic substance, acetaldehyde, is formed but it is so rapidly broken down that no ill effects are felt. When a person drinks on top of antabuse, this process is blocked, so that the acetaldehyde from alcohol is only slowly broken down and its level in the blood rises. Accumulating acetaldehyde brings about a sequence of physical sensations which each patient learns for himself. The patient learns what his particular response is because he is given a *test reaction* by the doctor at hospital. The purpose of this is not only to teach him what to expect but also to enable the doctor to cut the reaction short if it is unduly severe. The patient takes a tablet each morning for at least three days and is then given two to four ounces of spirits. The reaction begins about ten minues after taking alcohol and lasts about an hour. If unduly distressing it can be promptly terminated by drugs which counteract the unpleasant effects. The aim of the test is not to terrify the person taking it (this is in no way an 'aversion' treatment), but to let him learn from personal experience how he can use antabuse to stop drinking. He is prevented from drinking by the knowledge that alcohol will no longer achieve its pleasurable effect.

No patient should use the drug unless he has had an antabuse test. The first symptom to occur in the antabuse–alcohol reaction is flushing and warmth of the face. Then a pounding is felt at the temples as the heart beat accelerates. A headache commonly develops. Another common effect is a catch in the breath, as if there is some sort of obstruction in the windpipe; there may be coughing or a choking sensation. The patient becomes uncomfortably aware of his breathing because he has to work harder to take in the necessary air. There is generally an emotional accompaniment to the reaction; this is probably a direct effect of the acetaldehyde in the circulation, which may produce an anxious feeling.

The effects of antabuse occur if alcohol is taken within about three days after a tablet is taken. Once this period has elapsed, and the drug has been totally excreted from the system, no further adverse reactions will occur with drinking. The treatment plan calls for one tablet to be taken every morning. The bottle should have its unvarying place with the shaving kit or on the breakfast table and every morning the tablet may thus be taken without deliberation or inner debate. To those who protest against placing reliance on a pill rather than on will-power, alcoholics who have found antabuse a worthy aid reply that they use their will power to remember to take the tablet every morning.

Those helped most by antabuse are the alcoholics who for many months after becoming abstinent continue to have strong craving for alcohol. They emphasize eloquently that they regularly want a drink very badly indeed. For them antabuse provides a sort of chemical guard. The real value to the abstinent alcoholic of an antabuse régime is that in the event of a crisis which he is tempted to resolve through drinking he will have to wait for three days while antabuse is being eliminated from the system. By then he may have taken steps to resolve the difficulty, and decided to resume the antabuse instead of his drinking. In the early stages of treatment antabuse may be relied on heavily by patients who can scarcely believe that it will prove possible for them to remain abstinent by their own efforts. They feel they cannot undertake never to use alcohol again and are reassured both by the knowledge that, temporarily at any rate, it is impossible for them to drink, and also, paradoxically, by the information that they have only to leave off antabuse for three days, and it will be possible for them to drink again should such relief become imperative.

Occasionally antabuse itself, even if the patient does not drink, may produce mildly unpleasant effects in certain individuals who are hypersensitive. These effects include skin rashes, a state of lethargy, headache, a metallic taste in the mouth, stomach discomfort and, rarely, a confusional episode. Such reactions, although infrequent, are another reason why the drug should only be used under experienced medical supervision. The reactions can be treated easily, and other drugs similar in action to disulfiram may be substituted. Abstem (citrated calcium carbimide) is the most widely used alternative to antabuse.

Antabuse, correctly used, reduces the likelihood of impulsive drinking. It is only part of a comprehensive treatment programme but for some patients it may be lifesaving. These people consider that only the daily antabuse tablet, the antabuse habit, stands between their present sobriety and the resumption of uncontrolled drinking. Once having taken the tablet they have made their decision for that day. At a time when temptation is lowest they protect themselves against craving that might arise later on, for instance from the otherwise overwhelming attraction of the smell that wafts towards them from an open public-house door as they pass along the street.

How long should the automatic taking of antabuse continue? Six months, a year, for ever? No general answer can be given. Some give up the tablets soon and stay well. Often discussion makes it clear that the patient considers stopping antabuse at a time of particular strain, such as trouble at work or disturbance in a personal relationship. Of course this is just the time not to stop. The decision is best made jointly by patient and physician. It is important to make sure that the patient's decision to do without does not coincide with his turning over in his mind the possibility that he might be one of those legendary alcoholics who just conceivably could risk an occasional drink.

There is no justification for supposing that only the weak require antabuse, and that to use it is to rely on a crutch. Each patient's alcoholism is an individual matter. Some alcoholics electing to rely on antabuse are among the most resolute and self-explorative patients we have known. They view antabuse as an important medical discovery (they only wish that a drug was also discovered which could reduce the discomfort of craving). They use the analogy that if one were entering malarial country one would take prophylactic quinine; for them, going about the streets is to venture into disease territory.

Because antabuse may be bought over the counter of a chemist's shop three warnings should be given. It is unwise and may be extremely dangerous to start taking antabuse without having been physically examined and without having had a trial reaction watched by a doctor. After having had some drinks it is unsafe to take antabuse until the alcohol has been eliminated from the body; generally it is wise to wait twenty-four hours after the last drink. Lastly, the alcoholic has to know that he is on tablets; to do as some wives have done and give antabuse to someone surreptitiously is not only misguided but dangerous.

PSYCHOTHERAPY

The keystone of medical treatment is the adoption of a psychological approach which relies on discussion between patient and doctor. Someone who has become dependent on alcohol invariably has conflicts and problems which call for psychological measures. Individual psychotherapy, where the doctor and patient meet alone and regularly, is designed to help the latter appreciate the basis of the difficulties he has in his social relationships. Psychological treatments seek to identify the patient's misconceptions, and enable him to modify his behaviour. The patient may have used alcohol expressly to relieve distressing symptoms: anxiety experienced when required to speak in work discussions or meetings, lack of confidence in ability to do his job adequately, insecurity in relation to more senior people, conflicts in the marriage relationship. Instead of needing to relieve the symptoms with alcohol the patient is enabled to understand and control them.

The more long-term aim of psychological treatment is to bring about personality change. The patient gradually defines the personality problems which he had sought to alleviate by the use of alcohol. The psychiatrist helps the patient to grasp the distortion in his attitudes which bring about the difficulties. The patient then can himself go about restoring his affairs to order. If he fears that he is going to lose his job the psychiatrist does not intervene by going to see the employer. Instead, the patient and he study the patient's inadequacy feelings, his dependence on more forceful men in place of reliance on his own abilities, and irrational fears of punishment for supposed errors. The insights gained permit him to distinguish the realities of his situation from irrational fears that arise from past experiences but are currently distorting his personal relationships.

Many alcoholics are not responsive to the concept that their drinking is an attempt to repair a deep-seated personality disturbance; they fight shy of an individual treatment relationship with a psychiatrist. From them an alternative method of treatment must be sought.

Group Psychotherapy

An interesting development during recent years has been the finding[1] that group psychotherapy is effective with alcoholic patients. The members of a treatment group, generally about ten alcoholics, meet with one psychiatrist for sessions of an hour and a half each week, for about a year. The psychiatrist who has chosen patients whom he considers suitable to form a particular group conducts the meetings so as to evoke group interactions which bring about personality changes.

A group session consists of the descriptions by members of their recent experiences, each one speaking as he wishes, when he considers he has an idea to contribute to the discussion.

As the weeks pass, the members of the group report and pool their experiences; small triumphs are noted and disasters are shared, not only with interested attention but with responsible concern, because any member's setback is thoroughly understood and had perhaps even been anticipated. When a member has a lapse and begins to drink, the skills developed by the

1. Gleidman, L. H. (1958). 'Some contributions of group therapy in the treatment of chronic alcoholism'. In *Problems of Addiction and Habituation*, ed. Hoch, P. H. and Zubin, J. New York: Grune & Stratton. Also: Walton, H. J. (1961). 'Group methods in the psychiatric treatment of alcoholism'. *American Journal of Psychiatry*, *118*, 410.

group are put to the test; understanding, firmness in reaching sound decisions, and skill in communicating them often help the drinking member to recover rapidly without incurring serious harm.

The alcoholic in a group is able to try out new ways of approaching people, secure in the knowledge that the reactions of fellow members, whether appreciative or critical, will never be scornful or humiliating. They can tell him things that he will not tolerate hearing from non-alcoholics, because of their personal experience of the illness. Moreover, he knows that the psychiatrist conducting the group will control the development of individual or group emotions too threatening or too disruptive for the members themselves to handle. The psychiatrist trained in group methods conducts the meetings so as to foster therapeutic interactions, and to ensure that harmful developments are recognized in time and counteracted. His role does not call for domination of the group nor for giving advice. The group collectively works through the conflicts of opinion between members which arise as private preoccupations are disclosed and discussed.

As he gains in self-confidence, the unassertive alcoholic discovers that to express himself forcefully does not incur the catastrophes he had previously feared. In this way patients learn to understand the motives for their behaviour and develop ways of modifying them when they are unrealistic. Their chances of remaining abstinent are greatly strengthened even when difficulties supervene.

A former accountant in a group found employment as timekeeper on a building site. He had taken care to let his employers know of his alcoholism. His foreman told him to mark as present a man whom he was using elsewhere illicitly. This happened repeatedly. The patient discussed his difficulty in his treatment group; as he saw it, he would have to refuse. He was certain the foreman would see to it that he lost his hard-found job. The group members sympathetically agreed that here was a perplexing problem; but although individual members offered particular advices the consensus was that he should do what the foreman instructed. He did the opposite. His rebellion against the group's opinion was a try-out for subsequent rebellion against the foreman. He said to the foreman he was not happy about marking the absentee present. 'You do as I tell you,' said the foreman threateningly. Very unhappily he obeyed. But his protest was successful. The foreman never again asked him to be dishonest. This achievement gave him the confidence he needed to tell his employers that he was really capable of a more exacting job.

During the course of a group session problems will be focused upon, generally arising out of a recent situation related by one member, who also tells how he reacted to it. This becomes a theme in the discussion and it is worked upon from all sides. A patient described a lapse into drinking: 'I fell away last week. I'm having trouble with my daughter. I'd finished my antabuse and intended to get more at last week's meeting.' His wife, he said, had urged him to take their daughter to task. At first she had supported him when he began to reprimand the girl but then, 'as she usually does when she thinks I become too harsh with the children, my wife changed over and sided with my daughter. I couldn't stand that. I went out, had a couple of whiskies, and then came home to continue the brawl.'

Mr Peel said that he also had difficulty with his children because he was not sure how to deal with them.

'You can't dictate to young people today,' said Mr Fox. 'They think for themselves. You can't tie them down, especially the girls.'

Mr Walpole, the original speaker, could not accept this: 'I'm not going to stand for it. If she comes back home late again she'll find the door shut.' 'What right have we to judge our children?' asked Mr Fox, and the group went on to consider, some of them for the first time, how their children might understandably be confused by not knowing what value to place upon admonitions and controls exercised by a parent who until recently had been disorganized by drinking.

Mr Walpole admitted reflectively that his daughter had indeed been concerned about him when he was drinking. 'But,' he went on, 'a father *has* to exercise control. Once you let the children get on top of you, that's it.'

The group continued to discuss the position of the alcoholic parent. 'When you were drinking it didn't matter what time your daughter came in.' 'The child thinks: "He didn't care before, why should he care now?"' They insisted to Mr Walpole that aggressive handling of his daughter would fail. 'If you come the heavy father, she'll just go off.' A woman member, Mrs Holland, introduced a new note when she talked about her own youth. 'At sixteen I used to stay out late.' She said that, like Mr Walpole's wife, 'I want my husband to chastise the children if they do wrong, but when he does I take their side against him.' Several of the men then said that their wives also placed them in this false position. Mrs Holland, by identifying herself with Mr Walpole's wife, had taken on the role of all the missing spouses. But she was herself an alcoholic, so she could express the group's problem, which she did precisely: 'I tell my boy to be in by ten o'clock or there will be a row, and he answers back, "You weren't in by ten when you were in the pubs." Then there is chaos.'

Each member of the group had become enabled to see how his own actions in a common situation appeared to others, to wives and to children. Relationships in particular between parents and children were no longer seen as one-sided. Now they were putting themselves imaginatively in the position of their children, trying to see themselves from the outside. This led Mr Peel, whose father was also an alcoholic, to conclude with feeling: 'I mean to be different to my children than my father was to me.' The group had done its work for that session but the psychiatrist had registered a possible clue to Mr Walpole's intractable harshness to his daughter; he decided that he would provide an opportunity in a later session for Mr Walpole to discuss the treatment he had received from his father, which might be serving as a model for his own behaviour as a parent.

The group process does three things. It supports the recovering alcoholic in his abstinence by letting him see that he is wrong to think that an alcoholic is sinful and degenerate. When he perceives the strengths and positive capacities of his fellow patients, his disgust with himself also diminishes. When he sees that others accomplish what he feared was impossible for him he begins to believe that he can himself reorganize his life to exclude alcohol. Secondly it shows him the situations in which he repeatedly involves himself and which he characteristically mismanages so that he learns to deal with them more effectively. Lastly, the group member, by examining his and other members' ways of reacting and by exploring the origins of those ways, can in time modify his self-defeating patterns of behaviour.

ALCOHOLICS ANONYMOUS

The inspired plan to help alcoholics by enabling them to help other alcoholics was devised by a stockbroker, Bill W., and a medical practitioner, Dr Bob, at Akron, Ohio, in 1935. The movement was based on concepts and techniques derived from a number of sources. Both founders were active Oxford Group members and used as a basis for Alcoholics Anonymous the principles of open self-scrutiny, admission of defects, aid to others, and making reparations for harm done in the past. The religious component is epitomized by their adoption of an eighteenth-century prayer of Friedrich Ötinger: 'God give me the detachment to accept those things I cannot alter; the courage to alter those things which I can alter; and the wisdom to distinguish the ones from the others'; an AA member, in a phrase of William James, is asked in Step Two to believe that 'a Power greater than ourselves' can restore him to sanity. The

physician, W. D. Silkworth, proposed to the founders of the
movement the idea that alcoholism was an illness; his belief that
the basis of the condition was an allergy to alcohol was enthusi-
astically adopted and widely publicized.[1] This, as we have seen,
is no longer a tenable hypothesis, but it permitted an approach
to be formulated which identifies the drinking itself as the
disease process. Stopping drinking and remaining abstinent
are the goals of AA members. In their theoretical statement of
the causes of alcoholism they do not adopt the broader approach
of the medical profession, which holds that there are underlying
psychological factors to which attention must be paid.

Their programme is based on the famous Twelve Steps:

We –

1. Admitted we were powerless over alcohol – that our lives had
   become unmanageable.
2. Came to believe that a Power greater than ourselves could restore
   us to sanity.
3. Made a decision to turn our will and our lives over to the care
   of God as we understood Him.
4. Made a searching and fearless moral inventory of ourselves.
5. Admitted to God, to ourselves, and to another human being, the
   exact nature of our wrongs.
6. Were entirely ready to have God remove all these defects of
   character.
7. Humbly asked Him to remove our shortcomings.
8. Made a list of all persons we had harmed and became willing to
   make amends to them all.
9. Made direct amends to such people wherever possible, except
   when to do so would injure them or others.
10. Continued to take a personal inventory and when we were
    wrong promptly admitted it.
11. Sought through power of prayer and meditation to improve our
    conscious contact with God as we understood Him, praying only
    for knowledge of His will for us and the power to carry that out.

1. Silkworth, W. D. (1937). 'Alcoholism as a manifestation of allergy'.
Medical Record, *145*, 249.

12. Having had a spiritual experience as a result of these steps, tried to carry this message to alcoholics and to practise these principles in all our affairs.

These steps are buttressed by twelve 'Traditions', which are concerned with the cohesion and management of local groups. The first tradition is: 'Our common welfare should come first; personal recovery depends on AA unity'. The fifth tradition runs: 'Each group has but one primary purpose – to carry its message to the alcoholic who still suffers'. The ninth takes us firmly into the organizational sphere: 'Alcoholics Anonymous has no opinion on outside issues; hence the AA name ought never be drawn into public controversy'.

To join, all one has to do is to get in touch with any AA member or to look them up in the telephone directory. It is not necessary to have stopped drinking. The alcoholic who joins an AA group is provided with a new sub-culture, made up of companions engaged upon a common task.[1] A new, all-embracing outlook on life is offered him. He learns a special, memorable, technical language in which to talk about and reflect on the symptoms occurring in the course of alcoholism and he absorbs a system of ideas devised by alcoholics themselves to provide practical ways of becoming abstinent. Anybody who wants to stop drinking and is prepared to admit that he is 'powerless over alcohol' can join AA. There are groups in most cities. At the meetings members describe their successes and failures since the last meeting and discuss difficulties common to all. A new member may be introduced and absent members may be inquired about. One or more members usually will relate the story of former drinking days and successful recovery. Only alcoholics play a part in the movement, which does not rely on doctors or ministers or other professional personnel. Wives are admitted to special meetings.

As the designation of Alcoholics Anonymous emphasizes,

1. Bales, R. F. (1944). 'The therapeutic role of Alcoholics Anonymous'. *Quarterly Journal of Studies on Alcohol*, *5*, 267.

first names only are used, so that members can shed some of the
customary social caution (in English AA groups more stress
than in North America is placed on the anonymity principle).[1]

Each newcomer is assigned a sponsor, an AA member who
has successfully stopped drinking. The function of the sponsor
is to come to the sufferer's aid whenever necessary and to stay
with him for as long as necessary. The care and selflessness
shown by some sponsors is one of the twin pillars of the movement, the other being the group meetings, which may occur as
often as every night.

The success of different AA groups in providing active spon-
sorship for new members and in dealing with rivalries, open
hostilities and other quarrelsome behaviour varies from group
to group.[2]

The alcoholic who succeeds with AA's help in becoming
abstinent has found a constant body of people who share his
enduring interest to stay sober regardless of difficulties which
crop up. The discovery of so many pleasant men and women in
the group helps him considerably in ridding himself of the idea
that alcoholics, himself in particular, are despicable. His own
self-esteem grows with this realization. He finds friends, an
active social life, the satisfaction of helping others and, in time,
the chance to take a leading part in the affairs of his local group.
His guilt over the harm he did to others is reduced both by the
relief of confession and by the opportunities for reparation
which he is afforded when called upon to sponsor new members.
Many AA members find that the movement becomes their overriding life concern.

The AA approach can be a life-changing experience for
alcoholics who are sociable, who derive satisfaction from help-

1. Jellinek, E. M. (1960). *The Disease Concept of Alcoholism*, p. 185. New
Haven: College and University Press.

2. Maxwell, M. A. (1962). 'Alcoholics Anonymous, an interpretation'.
In *Society, Culture and Drinking Patterns*, ed. Pittman, D. J. and Snyder, C. R.
New York: John Wiley & Sons, Inc.

ing fellow sufferers and from their company, who are responsive to concentrated attention upon drinking and who do not seek psychological exploration and treatment of underlying problems. Nowadays AA groups will even receive alcoholics who are simultaneously undergoing psychiatric treatment; they are progressively willing to accept that some of their members are helped by medical measures such as antabuse; many groups have active links with physicians in their area, who provide hospital facilities for treating alcoholics during withdrawal symptoms. In some psychiatric hospitals AA members are invited in to sponsor patients being treated for alcoholism. One such hospital,[1] Warlingham Park Hospital near London, arranged for an AA group to function in the hospital itself. The physician can learn much from Alcoholics Anonymous and medical men interested in alcoholism do well to seek the co-operation of the local AA group.

AA achieves least success with those alcoholics who are not gregarious and cannot tolerate the pressures towards continuous and intimate relationships with others. Such alcoholics mention this as one of their chief reasons for not having been helped by the movement. Another is the distaste that may be engendered not only by having to confess publicly about their drinking history but also by the apparent relish with which, one after another, hardened abstainers recount their past and rehearse their former drinking habits.

These activities together with the religious emphasis, which varies considerably from group to group, put off some newcomers who feel themselves not part of the group. They are undoubtedly features which may strike an outsider attending an open meeting as unacceptable; however, the movement is not intended for outsiders but for insiders. It has forged techniques which it has found effective for many alcoholics. AA realizes for instance that public declarations of former

1. Glatt, M. M. (1961). 'Drinking habits of English (middle-class) alcoholics'. *Acta Psychiatrica Scandinavica*, *37*, 88.

drinking are a necessary group defence against relapse by serving as a constant reminder of what might happen again.

Two other forms of treatment which we do not personally use should be discussed.

AVERSION TREATMENT

Some physicians treat alcoholism by a method of *conditioning*. The essential of such a procedure is to induce in the patient an extremely unpleasant sensation in response to the taste, smell, and sight of alcohol. We will describe the most commonly used method, employing the drug apomorphine. This has only one important medical property: when injected it acts on the brain centres to produce vomiting.

Treatment consists in giving the patient alcohol in conjunction with an injection carefully timed so that nausea begins very shortly after the drink is taken and the patient vomits. The procedure is repeated several times in the course of a treatment session and half a dozen sessions take place over the course of about a fortnight. By the end of the conditioning course the patient has built up nauseating associations to the smell, taste, and gastric effects of alcohol. The conditioning stimulus of apomorphine is no longer necessary. He develops nausea whenever he handles a drink. In order to reinforce the conditioning, further treatment courses are advised, initially at six-monthly intervals but less frequently later on.

The treatment is drastic. It can only be administered under strict medical supervision since it is necessary that means should be available for combating collapse in those few patients who may be prostrated by the vomiting. Emetine is another drug sometimes used to induce vomiting.

More recently other agents have been used to produce a conditioned response. Patients have been induced to associate the effects of drinking with the pain of electric shocks or with sudden muscle paralysis which follows the injection of muscle-relaxants of the curare type.

While the emetic methods are practised widely in, for example, Poland and Russia,[1] clinicians in Britain and in North America have not been drawn to the use of methods which involve submitting their patients to unpleasant and painful procedures. There are other forms of medical treatment, surgery for instance, in which the patient is necessarily hurt but the doctor tries to minimize the pain as much as possible. In aversion treatment the suffering of the patient is deliberately brought about by the doctor. Alcoholics who submit to this treatment must be prodigiously well motivated to overcome their addiction. In Britain it is chiefly practised outside the National Health Service. The chief exponent of aversion therapy in the United States, who uses apomorphine, claims recovery for half his patients, who come mostly from the upper social classes and were able to pay for private treatment.[2]

The growing interest and knowledge in the field of behaviour therapy as a whole is likely to lead to a renewal of interest in aversion treatment. There is no doubt that it is quick, that it is safe under controlled conditions, and that it is based on a consistent psychological theory resting on firm experimental evidence. On the other hand, many physicians will continue to find it unacceptable and it ignores all the psychological factors determining alcoholism.

HYPNOSIS

Alcoholics sometimes ask to be treated by hypnosis and this has been employed by a few physicians. The basis of the method is to suggest to the alcoholic either that he does not enjoy

1. Chafetz, M. E. and Demone, H. W. (1962). *Alcoholism and Society*. New York: Oxford University Press.

2. Lemere, F. and Voegtlin, W. L. (1950). 'An evaluation of the aversion treatment of alcoholism'. *Quarterly Journal of Studies on Alcohol, 8,* 261.

drinking or else that drink makes him sick. Such suggestions, however, do not prove to be lasting and there can be few if any alcoholics who have been permanently helped by treatment which depends principally on this approach.

THE PROPER COURSE OF ACTION

Now that we have reviewed the types of treatment that are available or should be, we can see how an alcoholic may take stock of his position once he has realized that he is addicted and that he needs help to recover. What steps can he take? He can contact the local branch of AA or go to his doctor and state his problem bluntly. Nor should he be satisfied until he is receiving expert care. He should expect a general hospital to undertake all the treatment of his physical complications and to accept him as a patient during the 'drying-out' process when he first stops drinking and withdrawal symptoms occur. He should expect the psychiatrist who becomes responsible for his subsequent hospital management to design a programme to suit the requirements of his case. This should offer during the period of in-patient care a positive approach to alcoholism, in which the skills of psychiatrist, psychiatric social worker and nursing staff are each deployed. It is of the greatest importance that every alcoholic should be enabled to learn the facts about alcoholism as an illness.

During the subsequent out-patient treatment the same personnel will consolidate his treatment gains. They will help him further to achieve the personal integration that will enable him to lead his life profitably without further recourse to alcohol. If he should suffer a relapse he is entitled to expect that the medical staff concerned will not give him up but will rally to his support with a renewed offer of their resources.

If he does not find all this, he is not getting the treatment his illness deserves.

Chapter 11

RESULTS OF TREATMENT

WHAT are the chances of an alcoholic stopping drinking? We have seen that involuntary abstinence is fairly simply achieved by placing the drinker in hospital or prison. Unfortunately there are no figures to tell us whether any of these people remain abstinent afterwards but experience suggests that there must be very few such cases indeed. Temporary compulsory removal from sources of supply is not of itself an effective treatment for alcohol addiction.

Many alcoholics stop drinking with the help of Alcoholics Anonymous. Here again, the very nature of the organization necessitates that no statistics of recovery rates exist.

We can, however, obtain some information from reports of the success or failure of medical treatment. Abstinence is the customary and indeed the only practical yardstick of success that can be used in investigations following up treated alcoholics. With care it is possible to determine fairly reliably whether or not a patient is drinking at all.

Patients who were given no more than custodial care in a mental hospital were followed up six years later; of 98 who had been committed to Michigan Hospital 18 were found to have become abstinent and a further 16 were drinking only 'moderately'.[1]

When planned treatment is provided, the outcome is better. Davies and his colleagues[2] studied 50 cases at the Maudsley Hospital in London, where treatment of alcoholics is provided

1. Selzer, M. L. and Holloway, W. H. (1957). 'A follow-up of alcoholics committed to a state hospital'. *Quarterly Journal of Studies on Alcohol*, *18*, 98.

2. Davies, D. L., Shepherd, M., and Myers, E. (1956). 'The two-year prognosis of 50 alcoholic addicts after treatment in hospital'. *Quarterly Journal of Studies on Alcohol*, *17*, 485.

in a ward admitting all types of psychiatric patient; the treatment plan was geared to the individual patient's requirements;
group psychotherapy was not employed. Out-patient treatment on a supportive basis was provided. Two years later, 18
per cent were found to be totally abstinent, and another 18 per
cent had been abstinent for most of the time. Forty-two per cent
of the patients had maintained their social efficiency despite light
or heavy drinking.

Glatt[1] reported on 150 patients treated as voluntary patients
at Warlingham Park Hospital near London. A third of his
patients became totally abstinent. Another third relapsed,
usually within six months, but could be rated as improved. A
third of the patients were treatment failures.

Rathod and his colleagues,[2] also working at Warlingham
Parkland using group methods, followed up patients two years
after discharge. They had strongly advised all patients to
attend AA meetings regularly; however, a majority of the
patients who remained abstinent did not do so; instead, on their
own initiative they made frequent contact with the hospital staff.

There are pointers to the types of patients most likely to
succeed in treatment. Men do better than women, and older
men better than younger men. Social stability, especially having
a job, is associated with a good outcome from treatment.
Married people do better than those who are single or divorced.
Patients with psychopathic personality disorder, anti-social
people who experience little subjective distress themselves but
cause others to suffer, respond poorly to treatment. Those who
are well motivated for treatment are more likely to become
abstinent; therefore, patients who seem to the treatment staff to
be lacking in cooperation, who surreptitiously drink while in

1. Glatt, M. M. (1959). 'An alcoholic unit in a mental hospital'. *Lancet, ii*,
397.
2. Rathod, N. H., Gregory, E., Blows, D. and Thomas, G. H. (1966).
'A two year follow-up study of alcoholic patients'. *British Journal of
Psychiatry, 112*, 683.

hospital, and who do not respond constructively to psychological explorations are more likely to relapse into drinking after treatment. Wolff and Holland[1] in Cape Town showed that if an alcoholic is going to respond well to treatment he is more likely to do this on his first admission to a well-designed treatment service than on readmission. Readmission to this service was a feature of young alcoholics.

However, individual patients do not necessarily comply with these predictions. Some patients who are not cooperative, who resist efforts of the treatment staff to help them, and who make no substantial modification in their pattern of living sometimes confound prediction by remaining abstinent.

There is reason to believe that the best therapeutic results can be obtained if treatment begins on an in-patient basis and is followed by planned regular out-patient treatment. This approach is in operation at the unit for treatment of alcoholism[2] at the Royal Edinburgh Hospital set up with a grant from the Nuffield Provincial Hospitals Trust.

Further progress will depend on the development of specific and varied treatment régimes, because patients' needs cannot all be suited by a uniform approach. There must also be research to determine which types of alcoholic are best suited by each type of treatment programme. Wallerstein at the Winter Veterans Administration Hospital in the United States divided a sample of 178 alcoholic patients into four groups, each group obtaining a different form of treatment felt to be most appropriate for him.[3] While there are deficiencies in the study (the method of the aversion treatment was faulty, for example, some patients obtaining alcohol only when already nauseous from the emetic injection), it showed that some patients do respond

1. Wolff, S. and Holland, L. (1964). 'A questionnaire follow-up of alcoholic patients'. *Quarterly Journal of Studies on Alcohol, 25*, 108.

2. Walton, H. J., Ritson, E. B. and Kennedy, R. I. (1966). 'Response of alcoholics to clinic treatment'. *British Medical Journal, ii*, 1171.

3. Wallerstein, R. S. (1957). *Hospital Treatment of Alcoholism*. London: Imago Publishing Co. Ltd.

to each of the different régimes. Wallerstein's impression was that antabuse treatment is particularly effective in patients with a predominantly obsessional type of personality; the patients who responded best to group hypnotherapy had a different character structure, described as passive and dependent.

There is need for considerable experiment with different treatment methods. Recently, for instance, it has been shown that to begin treatment on an intensive outpatient basis rather than admitting every patient to hospital may be effective.[1]

The more research there is in the area of treatment the better. At the moment many agencies with differing professional backgrounds and different orientations towards the care of the alcoholic all practise treatment without assessing their treatment results. Sometimes this may be unavoidable, as with Alcoholics Anonymous where the approach rests on anonymity, but often it is inexcusable; a treatment service seems quite prepared to practise its methods without apparently recognizing the need ever to question whether they are effective. In other places assessments are made with such lack of scientific rigour that their purported successes are not acceptable. For instance, many agencies do not follow up their treated cases. How can they know whether the alcoholics remained abstinent? With scarcely more sophistication, others have observed the remission rate as a percentage of those who responded to an inquiry, blithely ignoring those who had escaped their follow-up and, one must presume, were much more likely to have relapsed. If 200 alcoholics were treated, and a year later 50 out of the hundred whom you can trace have done well, you are justified in claiming a success rate of 25 per cent, not of 50 per cent.

It may be even more misleading to take the alcoholic's statements of sobriety at face value, without seeking corroboration. There are many agencies which depend for their admirable

1. Edwards, G. and Guthrie, S. (1967). 'A controlled trial of in-patient and out-patient treatment of alcohol dependency.' Lancet, 1, 555.

work on public funds and issue optimistic and nebulous reports of their successes, often providing an illustrative case history or two. They do a disservice by underplaying the difficulties in providing adequate treatment and in underestimating the seriousness of the disorder. In Britain, the few studies we have cited are almost the only follow-up studies which meet the requisite standards.

The clinical challenge in the next few years will be to set up services which responsibly carry out treatment approaches of specified types, accompanied by careful evaluation of the alcoholic patients treated and their subsequent progress. Only by providing therapeutic services and also undertaking operational research will more effective treatment of alcoholism be achieved.

Chapter 12

THE ABSTINENT ALCOHOLIC

THE ALCOHOLIC WHO NO LONGER DRINKS

ALCOHOLISM is best regarded as a chronic disorder with a marked tendency towards relapse. Prolonged treatment is therefore necessary. The 'cure' calls for total abstinence from alcohol. The alcoholic, this means, remains a vulnerable person even if he stops drinking. In some respects he must continue to regard himself an an alcoholic even though he has stopped drinking.

Abstinent alcoholics are found in many places. There are alcoholics in prison who are undergoing enforced sobriety; their drinking may have been the direct cause of their confinement, for imprisonment is the treatment meted out to a substantial proportion of alcoholics. They are abstinent under duress. The vast majority begin drinking as soon as they are released.

Alcoholics undergoing treatment in general hospitals are often untroubled by craving as long as they are confined to the ward, while being investigated and treated for the medical complications of their alcoholism. The physician who concentrates on their liver disease or stomach ulcer may be lulled into unwarranted confidence that their drinking problem has been mastered. Almost invariably, however, the addictive drinking will return when the patient leaves the hospital.

These immured alcoholics, effectively prevented by their circumstances from drinking, are not our principal concern in this chapter. We shall discuss those alcoholics who are now voluntarily abstinent, deliberately, as a necessary means to prevent a relapse of their illness. Most of them will previously have been helped by one of the means outlined in the previous chapter.

Some alcoholics owe their abstinence to the programme of Alcoholics Anonymous. By November 1937, two years after its founding, Bill W. and Dr Bob could report that recovery, or 'sobriety', to use their term, had been achieved by 40 alcoholics. The abstinent AA member adheres to the Twelve Steps, reminding himself always that he is 'powerless over alcohol' and will never be able to drink again. It is the famous twelfth step, carrying the message to other alcoholics, that brings about the activity which becomes the most meaningful in many members' lives. They help other alcoholics to recover by drawing on their personal experience and understanding; this gives purpose and value to lives which had seemed hopeless and pointless. Every successful AA member has the 'key to sobriety', and the responsibility and privilege to help fellow sufferers. With justifiable pride and pardonable inaccuracy the fellowship proclaims that the 'world's best professionals' cannot help alcoholics to recover. The task falls upon AA members alone, the most strict of whom will not invoke the aid of physicians, ministers or social workers.

A number of medical clinics seek active collaboration with Alcoholics Anonymous; indeed some hospitals leave the after-care of patients solely to AA, no regimen of out-patient treatment being designed for the alcoholic after his discharge from in-patient treatment. Lack of staff may make this inevitable but a medical service which only advises AA attendance to out-patients is tacitly endorsing the AA claim that only the fellowship can keep alcoholics abstinent.

This is not so. Very many alcoholics who come to medical clinics have been to AA meetings but have not been able to derive benefit from the programme. It is not effective for every alcoholic or for every type of alcoholism. One of our patients put succinctly the objection that many feel: 'I tried AA for a year and found it a fascinating sociological phenomenon at first. But the masochistic bouts they indulged in over coffee appalled me, their reliving of their drunk-ups, getting up at meetings to purge themselves. The quality of evangelism I couldn't buy intellectually and that turned me away finally although I appreciated what it did for others.' Jellinek in his last book[1] pointedly warned: 'In spite of the respect and admiration to which Alcoholics Anonymous have a claim on account of their great achievements, there is every reason why the student of alcoholism should emancipate himself from accepting the exclusiveness of the picture of alcoholism as propounded by Alcoholics Anonymous.' Medical men whose sole provision for the aftercare of their patients is to recommend that they go to AA are remiss. Doctors, patients, and relatives should be clearly aware that the fellowship works best with compulsive alcoholics in whom enduring craving for alcohol is prominent. These will find in AA an effective method for remaining abstinent, and at the same time a social organization which can replace their harmful drinking associations.

The need that alcoholics have to find new social contacts in place of their former drinking relationships is sometimes the paramount problem of the abstinent alcoholic. Many never surmount it. Bacon[2] has analysed the stages by which membership of Alcoholics Anonymous enables the abstinent drinker to resume his place in society. First, he is dependent on a sponsor, who has twelve-stepped him during the faltering beginnings of his own sobriety. He becomes the confidant of the entire local group of alcoholics, hearing each confess publicly his own drinking history. In turn he may become a sponsor and can aspire to a prominent place in the group. Bales[3] has indicated

1. Jellinek, E. M. (1960). *The Disease Concept of Alcoholism*. New Haven: Hillhouse.

2. Bacon, S. D. (1957). 'A sociologist looks at Alcoholics Anonymous'. *Minn. Welfare, 10*, 35.

3. Bales, R. F. (1942). 'Types of social structure as factors in "cures" for alcoholic addiction'. *Applied Anthropology, 1*, 1.

that the alcoholic by temperament prefers multiple personal relations with emphasis on emotional expression; in Alcoholics Anonymous intense, emotional associations of a very intimate sort come about between members who share each others' woes and triumphs. The concept of AA which alcoholics find immediately helpful is the view that they suffer not from weakness or depravity but from a disease; that it is a disease from which one can recover is proved by the abstinent alcoholics whom he gets to know intimately.

Alcoholics Anonymous successes among the patients studied by the Connecticut Commission were recognized as having achieved a spectacular shift in their lives.[1] Interviewers considered that these abstinent AA members had acquired a sense of purpose and value in life. In the process they had become 'as dependent on AA as they were on alcohol'. The interviewers also remarked that many of the patients they studied had been unable to accommodate to the AA procedure.

The extension of treatment facilities in Britain will, we hope, mean that many more people will be enabled to stop drinking. These abstinent alcoholics will need the help of clinics to consolidate their treatment gains. No clinic is functioning adequately unless serious help is given to the patient who is rehabilitating himself socially. Responsible after-care is all the more important because of the finding that if an alcoholic remains abstinent for six months his future chances of continuing sobriety are very good. Davies, Shepherd and Myers[2] found that, of the treatment failures, 88 per cent recommenced their drinking within six, and nearly all within three, months of leaving the hospital. With only 20 per cent error, a patient's progress during the first six months indicates the state he will

1. Gerard, D. L., Saenger, G. and Wile, R. (1962). 'The abstinent alcoholic'. *Archives of General Psychiatry*, *6*, 83.

2. Davies, D. L. Shepherd, M. and Myers, E. (1956). 'The two-years' prognosis of 50 alcohol addicts after treatment in hospital'. *Quarterly Journal of Studies on Alcohol*, *17*, 485.

maintain during the next eighteen months and, generally, for considerably longer.

The task facing the recovered alcoholic is to stay off drink despite warm invitations by friends or gibes from the unsympathetic. In addition he will have to combat without alcohol the tensions produced by sudden hazards in his daily life, as well as those painful subjective feelings which are aroused by other people touching on vulnerable traits in his personality and exploiting, humiliating, angering or disappointing him. Even after months or years of abstinence the risk persists of his again resorting to drinking and thus precipitating a rapid return of his former addictive pattern.

Although many abstinent alcoholics cherish the lingering hope that they may be able to revert to normal social drinking, such a happy outcome almost never happens. The treated alcoholic who begins to drink again will almost certainly revert to his former drinking practices. Although Davies[1] has reported a few patients in his London series who were subsequently able to drink moderately this is an extremely rare contingency.

Symptomatic excessive drinkers (see page 88), of course, may after successful treatment of the underlying condition be able to drink again socially in a controlled way.

For many, the prospect of permanent abstinence is daunting. Alcoholics Anonymous recognizes and allows for this consternation by advocating that the abstinent alcoholic should think only about the next twenty-four hours, and resolve to negotiate only that stretch of time. Doctors who treat many alcoholics will have been chastened by the shudder and the pained look of reproof with which some alcoholics receive the information that they should never drink again. They prefer to plan only for the immediate future and for many this qualified

1. Davies, D. L. (1962). 'Normal drinking in recovered alcoholics'. *Quarterly Journal of Studies on Alcohol*, 23, 324.

resolve is the most realistic approach. If they have been modest in their undertaking they will not be completely demoralized by a relapse. The abstinent alcoholic who does lapse can often learn from his failure by appreciating the sort of conflict situation which precipitated the recurrence of drinking.

THE WIFE AND RECOVERY

When the husband is successfully treated and becomes abstinent this can gravely alter the family equilibrium. The competent wife who has become used to making all the decisions and to handling the finances of the family is not always ready to surrender these responsibilities to her spouse though he is eager to resume them. Justifiably she fears that, if he relapses, then once again he will plunge them all into chaos from which they were slowly and painfully rescued by her own exertions and resourcefulness. So much she will be prepared to say to the doctor or social worker, but she will be far less ready to admit that she does not want to shed an authority in the family which she has come to enjoy.

If she allows him scope to take up some responsibilities she will have to stand by and watch him flounder ineptly as he endeavours, for instance, to exert discipline over his children, when for years past he has been in no position to try. Should she intervene she may well start him drinking again. This very point was well illustrated in the group discussion which we quoted earlier. The wife must be particularly careful in her attempts to help him with his treatment. If, for instance, he should be taking an antabuse tablet each morning, what part should she play? She knows that trust is an important weapon for his successful treatment. If she insists on watching him take it, or even on dispensing it to him, then he will feel that she does not trust him but continues to regard him as sick and weak. If, on the other hand, she does not supervise the tablet-taking then she will blame herself should it later transpire that he has not had the tablets. The duties of consort and nurse are incompatible. She has to choose one role or the other and if she makes the wrong decision then everything will be undone. In general, AA members insist that her best approach is not to watch over him but to leave him alone. Psychiatrists consider the conditions that apply in each case with regard to the personalities of the individuals concerned.

For some wives the abstinence of recovered spouses is difficult to bear because the husbands become less active and socially more withdrawn. Their circle of drinking friends has been lost. Many a wife of an abstinent alcoholic confesses that she misses the gaiety of her husband's former drinking days. Now that he has recovered and she dares make comparisons again, he seems duller than her other friends. Nevertheless, usually she is content to sit with him at home in the unaccustomed calm of his sobriety. She feels that the battle he has won has been a joint victory.

Yet her peace of mind is never complete. All the time she knows that it is possible that he will break out again. Should he be late home she will begin to worry. If she cannot control her alarm she may start phoning the office for news of him or even send out the children to go and look in the local public houses. When he returns he is dismayed by her unconcealed agitation and concern. He realizes that she is surreptitiously sniffing his breath and her anxious regard signals to him that her trust in him is limited. Her anticipation of a relapse may actually precipitate one since we all of us tend to fulfil the expectations others have for us.

A wife came to hospital with her husband when he began to drink again, after being abstinent for seven months. She interrupted the information she was providing to turn to him and say: 'I tried to reach you all afternoon. I had a knot in my stomach since 5.30. I never moved from that window. My nails were down to the quick.' Panic-stricken waiting, the characteristic experience of the alcoholic's wife, had suddenly become a part of her existence once more.

Many a wife finds herself unprepared for the return of her husband's sexual potency. While he was drinking she had adjusted herself, first of all to intercourse being distasteful, then to its absence, which came as a relief. Now she is surprised by his renewed sexual ardour. She may not welcome it yet she feels that to deny her husband will invite doubts and even jealousy to reassert themselves. A sympathetic psychiatric social worker can help the wife to express and examine these very real difficulties and so work out what she must do.

THE ADJUSTMENT OF THE RECOVERED ALCOHOLIC

Abstinent alcoholics were studied by investigators working in the Commission on Alcoholism of the State of Connecticut.[1] In a group of 299 alcoholics, 55 were studied who had uninterrupted abstinence for as long as a year. Giving up drinking was associated with general all-round improvement; they enjoyed improved health, and better social, family and work relationships. The abstinent alcoholic looked better, felt better and viewed himself as a better person for being abstinent, and he was so regarded by others. But the investigators then undertook a closer examination into what they termed 'the nuances of their lives'. They classified the abstinent alcoholics into four sub-types. Half were *overly disturbed*: for them abstinence was sustained in a setting of tension, anxiety, dissatisfaction or resentment. A quarter were called *inconspicuously inadequate*: they showed what the interviewers rated as meagre involvement with life and living, an absence of any marked sense of purpose, interest or excitement. A third group (12 per cent) were the *successful AA members,* who had achieved a sense of purpose and

1. Gerard, D. L., Saenger, G. and Wile, R. (1962). 'The abstinent alcoholic'. *Archives of General Psychiatry, 6,* 83.

contentment through identification with the movement. A tenth of the abstinent alcoholics were named *independent successes*: they were self-respecting and seemed to have undergone personality growth with a resulting increased field of interest; they were not psychologically disturbed nor troubled by problems of resentment or aggression.

As this report makes clear, the alcoholic who has stopped drinking does not find things easy for him. The achievement of sobriety does not always bring with it tranquillity of mind. He finds that his former friends are not as ready as he is to believe that he has conquered his weakness. They are aware that the outlook for an alcohol addict becoming 'cured' is not good and, therefore, they deal with him warily. Some, indeed, prefer to keep clear of him especially if in the past he has let them down or embarrassed them. Though wives generally return to or welcome back their husbands when they have stopped drinking, the former alcoholic may find it more difficult to reclaim a place in the affections of his children. Their feelings have often been hardened, bitterly and for ever, by his behaviour during their most impressionable years.

He will have to decide whether he is strong enough to let new friends and new employers know that he used to drink, knowing that, if he tells, some of them may condemn him for it. He will have to decide how to avoid having a drink when one is offered. He is faced with numerous decisions which are all part of a large problem: should he try to return to the style of life he was attempting to lead when he began to drink excessively or should he start afresh on a new tack? Every former alcoholic will resolve this dilemma in his own way but to each one it is a crucial decision which has to be made painfully and with difficulty. Because of this, treatment of the alcoholic must aim at more than getting him to give up alcohol. It should endeavour to make him able to face the hazards of living that must still engage him.

Chapter 13

PUBLIC HEALTH ASPECTS OF ALCOHOLISM

THE DETERIORATED ALCOHOLIC

SOME alcoholics will not accept treatment. Others have been treated and the treatment has failed. The majority of both these groups continue to deteriorate mentally and physically and to become progressively disorganized socially. These people present a serious problem to the communities in which they live.

In many cities there are areas where down-and-out alcoholics gather. The Bowery in New York is perhaps the best known of the 'skid rows', a term used to indicate the slippery slope down which these alcoholics have fallen. Respectable citizens may not know the site of the skid row in their particular cities but the police are in no doubt. These areas are characteristically the cheapest lodging house areas of the city. The alcoholic spends his day in the street and, if he has the price of a bed, his night in the lodging house. If not, he sleeps under bridges or on derelict sites where he finds the company of fellows in the same state. Some clergymen offer such alcoholics nightly shelter in church crypts. Many of these men are meths drinkers. In skid row the alcoholic finds two desirable things: anonymity and the absence of society's strictures against drinking excesses. Alcoholics do not get to skid row from choice, but once there they may appreciate what it offers them. This is the chance to abandon themselves to drinking, immune from the shame resulting from the criticism of people who object and relatively unmolested by the police. These areas are eyesores and a matter for distress to the civic-minded. Nevertheless, they serve a purpose for society by providing a retreat for those who have extruded themselves when they gave up the struggle to remain socialized. Skid rows perform a function in the cities which generate them.

From any point of view skid row presents an important public health problem. Many people die there from the consequences of alcoholism. But even without this, since we now look upon alcoholism as an illness, these areas constitute reservoirs of ill people, in which affected men sink steadily and to which newcomers are constantly drifting. Skid rows cannot be dealt with by cleaning up the neighbourhood. Unless a more satisfactory solution is found for the individual concerned, the problem has not been tackled. Hostels are required, with sheltered workshops and energetic social welfare measures that might enable these men to return by degrees to health, cleanliness and self-respect. Without this, there is no hope.

Most communities do more than just tacitly providing a skid row area in their town. For alcoholics who will not make use of treatment services, for alcoholics who are irrecoverable, they provide some charity and care. This is generally through support for organizations which accept the challenge of helping seemingly hopeless cases, particularly those who are homeless and jobless. In Britain the Salvation Army must take most credit for this. Its hostels and its Officers have eased the existence of innumerable deteriorating alcoholics.

The Salvation Army has been impelled to enter the field of treatment as well. In a few places special homes have been set up, where alcoholics are accepted who show 'a sincere personal longing for deliverance'. Contact is kept with the men who leave by periodical letters and a monthly magazine. What started as a charitable concern for the destitute, based on religious precept, still remains so. But the workers have learned that care and charity by themselves are not enough. They have evolved a treatment orientation.

PRISON

Another measure which the community adopts to deal with alcoholics is *imprisonment*. Drunkenness is not itself an offence in Britain though people are still charged with being 'Drunk and Incapable' or 'Drunk and Disorderly'. Alcoholics are also picked up by the police for loitering and for vagrancy. First offenders get small fines for such offences but when they are often repeated magistrates send people to prison. Alcoholics are to be found in large numbers in most jails. Some alcoholics regard prison as a place of refuge. Food and shelter are provided there, devoid of any moralizing, which they feel they get from the Salvation Army, and without their being considered as mad, which is the impression they are sometimes given in psychiatric hospitals.

A study of alcoholics in prison was made by Jones,[1] who compared them with alcoholics who attended a clinic for alcoholism. The prisoners had much more unstable work records, poorer educational backgrounds and much more previous imprisonment. They had led impoverished lives devoid of gratification. Prison alcoholics were less commonly married and the marriages of those who were had not lasted.

Alcoholics often appear to have little wish to be treated[2] and look on the condition as wrong behaviour rather than as illness. Prison alcoholics have little motivation for treatment even if it is offered to them. Imprisonment is useless as a treatment for alcoholism. It is quite ineffective. Alternative approaches will have to be devised if the community wishes these people to be helped. It is important to recognize that, although alcoholics in prison may also have served sentences for other offences than drunkenness, such offences are usually a thing of the past. Prison alcoholics are most commonly committed

1. Jones, H. (1963). *Alcoholic Addiction*. London: Tavistock Publications.
2. Woodside, M. (1961). 'Women drinkers admitted to Holloway Prison'. *British Journal of Criminology*, January, 221.

because of their abnormal use of alcohol rather than for any palpably criminal behaviour.

An American study of men who were imprisoned for drunkenness[1] showed that on an average they had four non-inebriate arrests in addition. These non-alcoholic offences had taken place in their younger days, and had stopped when convictions for drunkenness began. Imprisoned for crimes to start with, they were subsequently jailed for public drunkenness.

While our concern in this book has been the alcoholic who is capable of recognizing his need for treatment and of responding to it, we do not want the responsibility of the community towards the more deteriorated alcoholics to be overlooked. We hope that, as treatment services become more adequate, less alcoholics will deteriorate to levels of helplessness. At present the need is to provide alcoholics themselves with understanding of possible paths to recovery and to serve upon responsible authorities most definite intimation that the proper place for alcoholics, however deteriorated they may be, is neither the gutter nor the jail.

SUICIDE

Many alcoholics kill themselves. The suicide rate for male alcoholics admitted for treatment in a London psychiatric hospital, for instance, was eighty-six times as high and for those who had been admitted to an observation ward was seventy-six times as high as for men in the same age groups in the general London population.[2] A Scandinavian study of 220 male alcoholics revealed that 7 per cent kill themselves during a five-year period after leaving hospital.[3]

1. Pittman, D. J. and Gordon, C. W. (1958). 'Criminal Career of the Chronic Police Case Inebriate'. *Quarterly Journal of Studies on Alcohol*, *19*, 11.

2. Kessel, N. and Grossman, G. (1961). 'Suicide in alcoholics'. *British Medical Journal*, *ii*, 1671.

3. Nørvig, J. and Nielsen, B. (1956). 'A follow-up study of 221 alcohol addicts in Denmark'. *Quarterly Journal of Studies on Alcohol*, *17*, 663.

Alcoholism has been termed chronic suicide by Menninger,[1] the inference being that alcoholics are really attempting to drink themselves to death. Other authors have also stressed the similarity in the disturbance of personality structure between alcoholics and suicides. 'An underlying personality disturbance which finally was brought to medical attention through an attempt at self-destruction had been previously evidenced for a prolonged length of time by the refuge in alcohol.'[2] Such notions are, of course, only speculative but every doctor who is responsible either for alcoholics or for people who deliberately poison or injure themselves knows how commonly the two are found in combination. In Edinburgh, 39 per cent of all men admitted to hospital having poisoned themselves were alcohol addicts or chronic alcoholics.[3] A study in St Louis[4] revealed that of 119 suicides where a history was available, 26 per cent had been chronic alcoholics. As long ago as 1900 reports were appearing showing that suicides rates were high in occupations where alcoholism was rife. A series of observations by Bandel[5] in different countries at different periods revealed close parallels between fluctuations in alcohol consumption and male mortality from suicide.

The importance of these findings from the public health point of view cannot be too strongly stressed. They indicate two things. Even the slightest intimation of suicidal intent by an alcoholic must be taken very seriously; also, a close watch must be kept upon all alcoholics before, during, and after treat-

1. Menninger, K. (1938). *Man against Himself*. New York: Harcourt, Brace.

2. Wallinga, J. V. (1949). 'Attempted suicide: a ten-year survey'. *Diseases of the Nervous System, 10,* 15.

3. Kessel, N. (1965). 'Self Poisoning'. *British Medical Journal, ii,* 1265, 1336.

4. Robins, E., Murphy, G. E., Wilkinson, R .H., Gassner, S. and Kayes, J. (1959). 'Some clinical considerations in the prevention of suicide'. *American Journal of Public Health, 49,* 888.

5. Summarized by Freudenberg, K. (1931). *Klinische Wochenschrift, 10,* 606.

ment so that any suicidal intentions can be detected in time to
prevent tragedies. Even so, some will not be preventable because
the suicidal impulse can arise very suddenly in association with
intoxication. The clinical impression is that, if the addiction is
cured, the risk of suicide is very considerably reduced.

ROAD ACCIDENTS

Road accidents are prominent and serious among the social
upheavals caused by drinking. The effect of alcohol upon driving performance has been extensively studied; there is progressive impairment in skill, judgement, and reaction time from the
first drink onwards.[1] The drinker himself becomes progressively less able to detect his own impairment. Apart from the
decline in driving performance the same release of inhibitions
which forms the social reason for drinking will affect the
drinker's driving style. He will not be content to remain behind
another car but will strive to overtake, dangerously if needs be.
Why should he give way to avoid an accident? Let the other
fellow do it. Too bad if the other fellow has also had a drink and
feels the same. In Britain the peak rate for road accidents co-
incides with the hour after the pubs close, when an army of
incapables is loosed on to the roads. Not all of these are drivers.
Drunken pedestrians also present a hazard. Every one of a
group of 64 pedestrians admitted to a Manchester Hospital
between midnight and 6 a.m. after being injured in a road accident was intoxicated.[2] It is reasonable to suppose that those who
were killed were in like state. But drunken drivers cause most
harm. Many workers have demonstrated conclusively the importance of a high blood alcohol concentration in drivers as a

1. Drew, G. C., Coloquhoun, W. P. and Long, H. A. (1959). 'The effect
of small doses of alcohol on a skill resembling driving'. *Medical Research
Council Memorandum*, No. 38. London: H.M.S.O.
2. Cassie, A. B. and Allan, W. R. (1961). 'Alcohol and Road Traffic
Accidents'. *British Medical Journal, ii*, 1668.

major factor in causing road accidents. In Toronto[1] the blood alcohol concentrations of 423 drivers involved in accidents were compared with those of other drivers who happened to pass the scene in approximately the same type of car at approximately the same time of day. Raised blood alcohol levels were consistently found more often in the drivers involved in accidents. A concentration of over 150 mg. per cent was found eight times more often among the 'accident' drivers. In a similar study[2] in the United States the ratio was thirty-three times more often. British figures for road casualties during the Christmas period of 1964 showed that in 44 per cent of fatal accidents at least one person concerned had consumed alcohol. Preston[3] considers that 500 deaths and between 2,000 and 3,000 serious injuries could be prevented annually in Britain if drivers and pedestrians did not go on the roads after drinking.

Of course, drunken drivers are not necessarily alcoholics. Indeed, the view has often been put forward that alcoholics are relatively harmless on the roads because they render themselves incapable of driving a car at all. Recently, however, incontrovertible evidence has been produced that alcoholics do get into trouble for drunken driving. This has been ably reviewed by Haddon.[4] Goldberg[5] found that known alcohol misusers (alcohol addicts, alcohol abusers and excessive drinkers, as defined by Swedish law) made up 41 per cent of the drunken drivers who had licences and 71 per cent of those

1. Lucas, G. H. W., Kalow, W., McColl, J. D., Griffiths, B. A. and Smith, H. W. (1953). 'Quantitative studies of the relationship between alcohol levels and motor vehicle accidents'. In *Proceedings of the Second International Conference on Alcohol and Road Traffic*, Toronto.

2. Holcomb, R. L. (1938). 'Alcohol in relation to traffic accidents'. *Journal of the American Medical Association*, iii, 1076.

3. Preston, B. (1958). *New Scientist*, 4, 1543.

4. Haddon, W., Jr (1963). 'Alcohol and highway accidents'. In *Alcohol and Road Traffic*, ed. Harvard, J. D. J. London: British Medical Association.

5. Goldberg, L. (1953). In *Proceedings of the Second International Conference on Alcohol and Road Traffic*, Toronto.

who had not. Schmidt[1] investigated driving accidents or
offences where alcohol was a factor and estimated that there
were 28 per cent alcoholics to be expected among all drivers
convicted for impaired or drunken driving in Ontario. A
corresponding study in Sweden has shown that 45 per cent of
men convicted for drunken driving can be classified as
alcoholics or problem drinkers.[2] Glatt[3] found that a quarter of
one group of driving alcoholics he studied and a half of another
had had past court appearances for driving under the influence.

In 1967 legislation came into force in Britain making it an
offence, with automatic revocation of driving licence, to drive
a car if the driver has an alcohol concentration of more than
80 milligrams in 100 millilitres of blood. Blood tests can be
demanded where a policeman has reason to believe that a driver
is under the influence of alcohol, and where a breathalyzer test
indicates that he has been drinking. During the first twelve
months in which this law has been operating there were 1,152
less road deaths than in the preceding year, a reduction of one
death in seven. There was also a 10 per cent reduction in road
casualties. The casualty rate was especially reduced (33 per cent)
between 10 p.m. and 4 a.m. The casualty figures for Saturday
night and early Sunday morning fell by 40 per cent.[4]

This blood level of 80 mg. per cent would ordinarily result
from drinking ten single whiskies or five pints of beer. Few
authorities are happy about such a high figure and most believe
that a concentration of 50 milligrams per cent – the equivalent
of three single whiskes, three half-pints of beer or a third of a
bottle of table wine – is the highest that could be accepted as
entirely consistent with safe driving. Of the drivers and motor
cyclists killed in December 1964 and January 1965, 38 per cent

1. Schmidt, W., Smart, R. G. and Popham, R. E. (1963). 'The Role of
alcoholism in motor vehicle accidents'. In *Alcohol and Road Traffic*, ed.
Harvard, J. D. J. London: British Medical Association.

2. Goldberg, L. op. cit.   3. Glatt, M. M. (1964). 'Alcoholism
in "impaired" and drunken driving'. *Lancet*, ii, 161.

4. Minister of Transport, reported in *The Times*, 12 December 1968.

had alcohol present in the blood. Three quarters of these had blood alcohol levels of 50 mg. per cent or more and over half had levels of 100 mg. or higher.

The evidence that a substantial proportion of those involved in drunken-driving offences are alcoholics should suggest to the authorities an additional profitable approach. This would be to institute a programme of routine evaluation of the alcoholism status of those brought before the Courts and the offering of proper treatment facilities when appropriate.

SOCIAL CONTROLS

In Britain, as in most Western countries, there are social controls placed on the use, and hence on the abuse, of alcohol. It may only be sold in licensed places for a limited number of hours each day and there is a tax on it. These measures undoubtedly restrict alcohol consumption and, as we have seen, it was the tightening of the licensing laws, first introduced into Britain in 1553, that curbed the excesses of the gin-palace era.

The government has to strike a balance between permitting the majority of citizens, to whom alcohol is no problem, the right to drink where and when they wish and its duty to limit misuse.

Licensing laws do control consumption. Following their relaxation in Sweden in 1955 the amount of spirits sold increased by a third; on the other hand sales of wine decreased by a fifth. Along with the increased consumption there was a marked increase in convictions for drunkenness. The number of alcoholics presenting for treatment steadily increased. In the following year the authorities raised the price of the commonest spirit by 20 per cent. There followed a diminished demand for this and the consumption of wine increased. Although this latter policy was successful, therefore, in reducing spirit drinking, in 1957 a further step was introduced; temperance boards listed persons known for their excessive drinking who were thereby barred from purchasing liquor.[1]

1. Skutin, A. (1959). 'Sweden, Sequel'. In *Drinking and Intoxication*, ed. McCarthy, R. G. New Haven: College and University Press.

Here, within the course of a few years, we have evidence of how first a change in licensing laws and then a change in taxation system each produced a modification in drinking habits.

Prohibition is the extreme form of licensing restriction. We have seen that its effects when it was tried in the United States are still disputed. Certainly no such action is thinkable merely to restrict the number of alcoholics. Indeed, when legislating concerning the sale and consumption of alcohol, alcoholism is only one of the factors that has to be taken into consideration. However, it is an important issue, and we believe that any measures, fiscal or other, which would limit the sales of spirits while favouring beverages like beer or wine would probably reduce the number of alcoholics.

Besides legislation, government and other agencies can influence the extent of alcoholism both by educational means (see p. 176) and by curbing excessively persuasive advertising by the drink industry, particularly where this is directed towards encouraging young people to drink.

RESEARCH

A great deal of research is still required before many of the fundamental questions of alcoholism will be solved. Research will have to be carried out in many different areas – biochemistry, pharmacology, clinical medicine, sociology, and public health. We list the most important areas of possible research. The studies we indicate are called for to provide answers to questions which arise in clinical practice.

Biochemical and Physiological Research

Studies to explore the body changes that take place in response to prolonged drinking.

Studies of alterations in the body's response to alcohol. Why are some people more prone than others to get withdrawal symptoms ? What is the mechanism whereby tolerance at first increases in alcoholics and later decreases ?

Are there other substances (so-galled congeners) present in alcoholic drinks which increase the effects of alcohol on the body?

Can chemical additives be developed which, though not altering the pleasurable effects of alcohol, will protect against the long-term effects?

Clinical Studies

Investigation of the course of alcoholism in the young.

The personality characteristics of alcoholics, especially the identification of patterns of behaviour which were present before the excessive drinking. What changes in personality are produced by the alcoholism itself?

Determination of the sub-types of alcoholism. Statistical studies of the course and outcome of the different varieties of alcoholism.

Stages in recovery from alcoholism. Why do some abstinent alcoholics adjust well while others remain poorly adjusted?

What is the incidence of physical illnesses attributable to alcoholism?

How frequent are the brain diseases attributable to alcoholism?

The investigation of alcoholism in women.

A systematic study of the effect of an alcoholic on his family.

What is the expectation of life of the established alcoholic?

Preventive Measures

The identification of pre-alcoholism, so as to be able to advise and protect vulnerable individuals before addiction develops.

The investigation of measures which will make excessive drinkers come forward for evaluation and treatment.

Whether an Information Service makes members of the community more understanding of, and helpful to, alcoholics.

What measures can be developed to influence social agencies (governmental, local authority, and voluntary) to adopt a more effective approach to alcoholics?

What are the effects of social controls – licensing, taxation, hours of permitted sale – on the incidence of both drunkenness and alcoholism?

What proportion of persons convicted of drunkenness are alcoholic? What proportion of those involved in drunken driving accidents are alcoholic? What effect would routine police tests of drivers involved in accidents and, for those convicted, stiffer penalties, such as imprisonment, have on reducing drunken driving?

Social and Cultural Factors

The study of the form and relative prevalence of alcoholism in different cultures and in different groups (e.g. ethnic, religious and social-class) within a single culture. These studies would be concerned with the prevalence of alcoholism within the various groups, the forms which it takes and the actions taken by the alcoholics themselves, their families and their social group to deal with the problem.

Estimation of the loss to industry through alcoholism.

Estimation of the economic cost of alcoholism. There is the cost of medical services, but there are also hidden costs which may well amount to a greater sum. The cost of absenteeism, the loss to firms of key personnel who become incapacitated at the height of their working powers, the cost of provision of children's care services, the cost of National Assistance to support the family.

Treatment Studies

Comparison of methods of dealing with withdrawal symptoms when the alcoholic stops drinking.

A comparison of methods of treatment for alcohol addiction. What are the success rates of the different medical methods of treatment? How do they compare with non-medical methods?

A similar comparison of treatment services designed to combat alcohol addiction.

MEDICAL SERVICES

According to the degree of development of a country its standards of medical care increase. Not only will better facilities be provided but the medical services will deal with an increasing range of abnormalities. A wider range of conditions will come to be regarded as illness. Neurotic illness is a case in point. In under-doctored countries such illnesses hardly enter the province of medicine. In Western countries they do, although the amount of available treatment services may be rationed by cost or by the waiting list. Where a national health service exists those responsible for its management have to set limits to its activities. These limits change from time to time and are always a subject of debate. At the moment the management of alcoholics falls at about the limit and certain illogicalities arise from this. Those who suffer the physical diseases resulting from alcoholism find treatment readily available for this part of their illness. Those who want to be treated for addiction are encouraged to seek medical help, while at the same time provision of this is so woefully inadequate that many are bound to be disappointed. When it comes to the management of acute intoxication or of the less severe consequences of alcohol withdrawal, the medical services show reluctance to be engaged at all. A man arriving at a hospital tremulous and agitated from alcohol withdrawal because he is trying to stop drinking, even though this may be a relapse after treatment to which he has responded very well, is likely to be denied the bed and the immediate care to which, in our view, he should be entitled.

An investigation in the emergency ward of the Massachusetts General Hospital in Boston[1] showed that the admitting doctors failed to diagnose as alcoholic more than half the

1. Blane, H. T., Overton, W. F., Jr and Chafetz, M. E. (1963). 'Social factors in the diagnosis of alcoholism. 1. Characteristics of the Patient'. *Quarterly Journal of Studies on Alcohol, 24,* 640.

patients who on strict medical criteria should have been so
diagnosed. The undiagnosed alcoholics, as compared to
patients where it was diagnosed, were more often referred to
the hospital by doctors, rather than by other agencies; they
more frequently had a job and more often were living with their
families. The diagnosed alcoholics, on the other hand, more
frequently were brought to hospital with a police escort. The
socially fortunate alcoholic, this investigation shows, is less
likely to have his disorder properly diagnosed. The authors
conclude 'from the physician's viewpoint, the alcoholic who is
medically ill but relatively intact socially is not an alcoholic'.
There is no doubt that a similar wrong attitude is found among
British physicians. 'We do not know what proportion of
patients coming to hospitals in Britain, not specifically for
alcoholic illnesses, are, in fact, unrecognized alcoholics. However, one in eight of 1,000 admissions to the medical wards of a
Melbourne hospital were recently shown[1] to be alcoholics. A
third of these were admitted with illnesses considered to be
directly related to excessive drinking and another fifth were
possibly related. The illnesses of the remainder were not con-
nected with their drinking except for 6 per cent whose admissions followed suicidal overdoses. These findings indicate that
careful history taking in the medical wards would disclose a
large number of alcoholics in need of treatment. Similar figures
from Connecticut have been reported.'[2]

Doctors in Britain still feel themselves at liberty to regard
alcoholism as a moral as much as a medical problem. The
American Medical Association since 1935 has taken a more enlightened viewpoint. Alcoholics are best served where there are
special facilities created for their management. The number of
these set up in Britain under the National Health Service can

1. Green, J. R. (1965). 'The incidence of alcoholism in patients admitted
to medical wards of a public hospital'. *Medical Journal of Australia*, *1*, 465.
2. Nolan, J. P. (1965). 'Alcohol as a factor in the illness of University
Service patients'. *American Journal of Medical Science*, *249*, 135.

still be counted on the fingers of one hand. In 1962, the Ministry of Health recommended in a memorandum to hospital authorities that treatment for alcoholism should as far as possible be given in specialist units.[1] The memorandum suggested that hospital boards that had not already established such units should do so, aiming initially at one in each Region and improving the position as necessary. This has not been implemented. Regional Hospital Boards must now be pressed to set up the services which are acknowledged to be necessary. Existing arrangements cannot be regarded as more than gestures towards a satisfactory medical service.

The corollary to this is that alcoholics do not approach medical men for help. Parr[2] has provided some interesting information on this subject, as a result of questioning 480 general practitioners about alcoholism in their practices. The prevalence of alcoholism thus determined was exceedingly low. Even more important, only a quarter of the cases general practitioners knew about had consulted for their excessive drinking and only a half of these had been referred for specialist treatment. A fifth of the doctors 'did not know of a single case of alcoholism in their practice'. A London doctor said that he had not had even one case asking for treatment in thirty years' practice. A doctor practising in a North Country town wrote: 'In twenty years I can only remember one case'. A partner in a group practice in a near-by town replied: 'We really do not have problems from alcohol in this town and it is some years since either a patient or a relative approached any of us in this practice for help in connection with alcoholism'. A factory doctor answered: 'In this factory we have some 12,000 employees and, after being eleven years working full time among them, I cannot think of any alcoholic within the meaning of the definition given.' (This was the W.H.O. definition, see page 18.)

1. Ministry of Health Memorandum, 1962.
2. Parr, D. (1957). 'Alcoholism in general practice'. *British Journal of Addiction*, *54*, 25.

It is difficult to believe these responses spring entirely from alcoholics' reluctance to approach a doctor. The latter's attitude must be of equal importance. For example, one doctor wrote to Parr: 'Generally speaking, I suggest alcoholics avoid doctors, and doctors in the main try to avoid alcoholics. Perhaps the parsons know more about the problem'. Such attitudes arise from inadequate medical training. Parr himself comments, 'I trained in a medical school of the highest academic repute but can only remember one mention of the subject, namely, when a lecturer on cirrhosis of the liver enjoined us to "find out why the man took to drink". This single sentence impressed itself upon us by its unexpectedness.'

EDUCATING AND INFORMING THE PUBLIC

If doctors themselves are only partially informed about alcoholism, how much less do people at large know about it? Public education will only come about as the result of a deliberate campaign to make information available. At the moment, in place of sustained provision of information, there are only sporadic newspaper articles and broadcasts. For every factual programme on alcoholism there are scores of dramas in which some leading character drinks excessively: the fanciful presentation of his plight and his too facile redemption do not help to convey the truth about the condition, particularly as alcoholism is never portrayed as a medical problem. This does not apply to the characterization of great writers, especially those with particular reasons for insight into the problem; the characters in *The Iceman Cometh* by O'Neill are in no way idealized but are recognizable to anyone familiar with alcoholism. When a celebrated alcoholic dies, a poet like Dylan Thomas, a novelist like Scott Fitzgerald or a playwright like Brendan Behan, there is an all too brief concern over alcoholism but soon the drinking which in fact killed is transmuted into part of the romantic legend. Ask yourself if you do not believe that alcoholism was in some way necessary for the creativity of these three writers. That such a view can be held is a measure of the ignorance that exists about drinking excesses, an error which the artist himself may share and even foster.

If alcoholics are to avail themselves of whatever treatment facilities are provided it is necessary to modify the prevailing attitude of society, which is scornful, unsympathetic, and morally condemning. While such attitudes persist it is difficult for the early alcoholic, still with a responsible place in society, to admit his condition. A very great advance that could be made in tackling the problem by public health methods would be the dissemination of factual information with sufficient force to displace harmful attitudes and to correct misconceptions. In the United States this has been tackled with characteristic vigour and great success. There are now public health programmes, backed by legislation, in the great majority of the separate States. A School of Alcohol Studies, established at Yale and now moved to Rutgers, has been in existence since 1932. It publishes the *Quarterly Journal of Studies on Alcohol,* the most important periodical on the subject. It is concerned both with research into problems of alcohol and with the provision of information; its annual summer schools are famous. In 1944, there were set up 'two free clinics for the guidance of inebriates' in Hartford and New Haven. The pattern of staffing of these 'Yale Plan Clinics' by psychiatrists, general physicians and social workers has been widely accepted as a model.

The United States National Council on Alcoholism was started at Yale in 1944. Its headquarters are in the New York Academy of Medicine building. Its impact was immediate; its message reached everywhere: 'Alcoholism is a disease and the alcoholic a sick person. The alcoholic can be helped and is worth helping. This is a public health problem and, therefore, a public responsibility.' The American N.C.A. is a voluntary organization with branches in every major city. The task of these branches is to stimulate the growth of treatment services, promote conferences, arrange lectures and spread information on alcoholism. They also provide assistance to professional and lay organizations in connexion with alcoholism.

In Britain a National Council on Alcoholism was established only in 1962. It is a national voluntary agency, organized by professional and lay people, and aims to stimulate the formation of local councils in urban areas, to function as information centres. The address of the National Council is 212a Shaftesbury Avenue, London, W.C.2.

A major undertaking of the British N.C.A. will be the setting up of Information Centres throughout Britain. (The first was opened in Liverpool in 1963.) These centres will be publicity organizations which will attempt to mobilize public action to improving treatment services for, and attitudes to, alcoholism. In addition they will provide accurate information to anyone interested. Alcoholics will be encouraged to come there to obtain advice about suitable avenues of treatment; members of their families will also be able to obtain guidance.

AA members are usually to be found playing an effective and knowing part wherever efforts are under way to improve public attitudes or to develop social or medical services for helping alcoholics.

In Britain, alcoholism has yet to become recognized as a problem which affects the community. Members of the community do not discharge their responsibilities merely by seeing to it that medical and social services are set up. Employers, for instance, carry individual responsibilities to their alcoholic employees. It would be an asset to them to realize that alcoholism is not a moral but a medical condition that is treatable. This knowledge will free them not only to act charitably but also to keep on their staff men of proven capability who if treated will continue to do useful work. If the employee shows evident willingness to have treatment for his condition it may be very much worth his employer's while to see that he gets it.

To end by considering alcoholism as a public health problem is right. It is a considerable problem, a much greater one than medical administrators or social strategists are yet prepared to admit. It is a health problem because alcoholism is an illness; a grudging admission of this is slowly being given by the medical profession. It is a public problem because the alcoholic embroils in his illness a large array of other people, not only his family and his friends, not only his employers and a number of social welfare workers, but also others, complete strangers. Each of us supports him if he needs National Assistance; some of us have to witness his anti-social behaviour; any of us may become involved in his accidents. Some of us may be confronted by his final misery. We cannot afford, therefore, to ignore him or his problems. Nor should we. He is a sick member of our society.

Society will continue to generate great numbers of alcoholics We do not yet know how to prevent this. Even if we did we might well be unwilling to adopt the appropriate measures, since they would very likely limit individual freedom by imposing legal or economic restrictions on the sale and consumption of drink. We already accept, with ill grace, restricted hours of sale and a heavy duty on liquor. If the price to be paid for reducing the number of alcoholics were to include steps that made it harder or more expensive for the large majority of normal, social drinkers to get a drink, would that be justifiable? Everyone has to make up his own mind about this.

But there is no such dilemma in deciding about the need for improvement of treatment services. To urge this is, at present, the most effective public action that anyone anxious to combat alcoholism can take.

Two things are required to produce an alcoholic: the drink and the person. Restriction of supply is a debatable matter but helping the vulnerable person by seeing that proper treatment is available and getting him to accept it is a civilized and a merciful act, open to us all.

BIBLIOGRAPHY

Advertising Inquiry Council (1961). *Report on Drink Advertising.* London. (P. 21.)

Åmark, C. (1951). 'A study in alcoholism'. *Acta Psychologica et Neurologica Scandinavica*, Supplement 70. (P. 107).

Annual Report of the Commissioners of Customs and Excise, 1962–63. London: H.M.S.O. (P. 47.)

Aronson, H. and Gilbert, A. (1963). 'Pre-adolescent sons of male alcoholics'. *Archives of General Psychiatry*, 8, 235. (Pp. 67, 117.)

Bacon, S. D. (1957). 'A sociologist looks at Alcoholics Anonymous'. *Minn. Welfare*, 10, 35. (P. 154.)

Bailey, M. B., Haberman, P. W. and Alksne, H. (1965). 'The Epidemiology of Alcoholism in an Urban Residential Area'. *Quarterly Journal of Studies on Alcohol*, 26, 19. (P. 20.)

Bales, R. F. (1942). 'Types of social structure as factors in "cures" for alcoholic addiction'. *Applied Anthropology*, 1, 1. (P. 154).

Bales, R. F. (1944). 'The Therapeutic Role of Alcoholics Anonymous'. *Quarterly Journal of Studies on Alcohol*, 5, 267. (P. 141).

Bales, R. F. (1946). 'Cultural differences in rates of alcoholism'. *Quarterly Journal of Studies on Alcohol*, 6, 482. (P. 50.)

Bastide, M. (1954). 'Une enquête sur l'opinion publique à l'égard de l'alcoolisme'. *Population*, 9, 13. (P. 45.)

Blane, H. T., Overton, W. F., Jr and Chafetz, M. E. (1963). 'Social factors in the diagnosis of alcoholism. 1. Characteristics of the Patient'. *Quarterly Journal of Studies on Alcohol*, 24, 640. (P. 173.)

British Medical Association (Scottish Office). *Memorandum of Evidence to the Standing Medical Advisory Committee's Special Sub-committee on Alcoholism*, May 1964. (P. 126.)

British Medical Journal Supplement, 1961, 1, 190. (P. 123.)

Cassie, A. B. and Allan, W. R. (1961). 'Alcohol and Road Traffic Accidents'. *British Medical Journal*, ii, 1668. (P. 166.)

Chafetz, M. E. and Demone, H. W. (1962). *Alcoholism and Society*. New York: Oxford University Press. (P. 145.)

Cohen, J., Dearnaley, E. J. and Hansel, C. E. M. (1958). 'The risk taken in driving under the influence of alcohol'. *British Medical Journal*, 1, 1438. (P. 27.)

Davies, D. L. (1962). 'Normal drinking in recovered alcoholics' *Quarterly Journal of Studies on Alcohol, 23*, 324. (P. 156.)

Davies, D. L., Shepherd, M. and Myers, E. (1956). 'The two-year prognosis of 50 alcoholic addicts after treatment in hospital'. *Quarterly Journal of Studies on Alcohol, 17*, 485. (Pp. 147, 155.)

Drew, G. C., Colquohoun, W. P. and Long, H. A. (1959). 'The effect of small doses of alcohol on a skill resembling driving'. *Medical Research Council Memorandum*, No. 38. London: H.M.S.O. (P. 166.)

Duchène, H., Schutzenberger, M. P., Biro, J. and Schmitz, B. (1952). 'Ages of couples where the husband is alcoholic'. *La Semaine des Hôpitaux de Paris, 28*, 1857. (P. 107.)

Edwards, G. and Guthrie, S. (1967). 'A controlled trial of in-patient and out-patient treatment of alcohol dependency'. *Lancet, 1*, 555.

Expert Committee on Mental Health (1951). *Report on the First Session of the Alcoholism Subcommittee*. W.H.O. Technical Report No. 42, Annex 2. (P. 18.)

Fenichel, O. (1945). *The Psychoanalytical Theory of Neurosis*. New York: Norton. (P. 77.)

Fox, R. (1956). 'The alcoholic spouse'. In *Neurotic Interaction in Marriage*, ed. Eisenstein, V. W. New York: Basic Books, Inc. (P. 115.)

Freudenberg, K. (1931). *Klinische Wochenschrift, 10*, 606. (P. 165.)

General Board of Control for Scotland (1957–62). *Annual Reports for the years 1956 to 1961*. Edinburgh: H.M.S.O. (P. 19.)

Gerard, D. L., Saenger, G. and Wile, R. (1962). 'The abstinent alcoholic'. *Archives of General Psychiatry, 6*, 83. (Pp. 155, 159.)

Glatt, M. M. (1959). 'An alcoholic unit in a mental hospital'. *Lancet, ii*, 397. (P. 148.)

Glatt, M. M. (1961). 'Drinking habits of English (middle-class) alcoholics'. *Acta Psychiatrica Scandinavica, 37*, 88. (P. 143.)

Glatt, M. M. (1964). 'Alcoholism in "impaired" and drunken driving'. *Lancet, ii*, 161. (P. 168.)

Gliedman, L. H. (1958). 'Some contributions of group therapy in the treatment of chronic alcoholism'. In *Problems of Addiction and Habituation*, ed. Hoch, P. H. and Zubin, J. New York: Grune & Stratton. (P. 135.)

Goldberg, L. (1953). *Proceedings of the Second International Conference on Alcohol and Road Traffic*, Toronto. (Pp. 167, 168.)

Green, J. R. (1965). 'The incidence of alcoholism in patients admitted to medical wards of a public hospital'. *Medical Journal of Australia, 1*, 465. (P. 174.)

Haddon, W., Jr (1963). 'Alcohol and highway accidents'. In *Alcohol and Road Traffic*, ed. Harvard, J. D. J. London: British Medical Association. (P. 167.)

Holcomb, R. L. (1938). 'Alcohol in relation to traffic accidents'. *Journal of the American Medical Association, iii*, 1076. (P. 167.)

Hopkinson, T. (1945). *The Pub and the People*. London: Gollancz. (P. 48.)

Horton, D. (1943). 'The functions of alcohol in primitive societies: a cross-cultural study'. *Quarterly Journal of Studies on Alcohol, 4*, 199. (P. 44.)

Hulton Readership Survey. Figures quoted by kind permission of The National Trade Press Ltd. (P. 49.)

Hyde, R. W. and Chisholm, R. M. (1944). 'Studies in medical sociology. III. The relation of mental disorder to race and nationality'. *New England Journal of Medicine, 231*, 612. (P. 50.)

Jellinek, E. M. (1960). *The Disease Concept of Alcoholism*. New Haven: Hillhouse Press. (Pp. 81, 142, 154.)

Jones, H. (1963). *Alcoholic Addiction*. London: Tavistock Publications. (P. 163.)

Kessel, N. (1965). 'Self Poisoning'. *British Medical Journal, ii*, 1265, 1336. (P. 165.)

Kessel, N. and Grossman, G. (1961). 'Suicide in acloholics'. *British Medical Journal, ii*, 1671. (P. 164.)

Knight, R. P. (1937). 'The psychodynamics of chronic alcoholism'. *Journal of Nervous and Mental Diseases, 86*, 538. (P. 78).

Lemere, F. (1956). 'The nature and significance of brain damage from alcoholism'. *American Journal of Psychiatry, 113*, 361. (P. 70).

Lemere, F. and Voegtlin, W. L. (1950). 'An evaluation of the aversion treatment of alcoholism'. *Quarterly Journal of Studies on Alcohol, 8*, 261. (P. 145.)

Lolli, G. E., Serianni, G. M. G. and Luzzatto-Fegiz, P. (1958). *Alcohol in Italian Culture*. Glencoe, Illinois: The Free Press. (Pp. 46, 51.)

Lucas, G. H. W., Kalow, W., McColl, J. D., Griffiths, B. A. and Smith, H. W. (1953). 'Quantitative studies of the relationship between alcohol levels and motor vehicle accidents'. In *Proceedings of the Second International Conference on Alcohol and Road Traffic*. Toronto. (P. 166.)

Malzberg, B. (1960). *The Alcoholic Psychosis*. Glencoe, Illinois: The Free Press. (P. 52.)

Mann, M. (1950). *Primer on Alcoholism*. New York: Reinhart & Co., Inc. (P. 112.)

Maxwell, M. A. (1962). 'Alcoholics Anonymous, an interpretation'. In *Society, Culture and Drinking Patterns*, ed. Pittman, D. J. and Snyder, C. R. New York: John Wiley & Sons, Inc. (P. 142.)

McCarthy, R. G. (1946). 'A public clinic approach to certain aspects of alcoholism'. *Quarterly Journal of Studies on Alcoholism, 6*, 500. (P. 127.

McCarthy, R. G. and Douglass, E. M. (1949). *Alcohol and Social Responsibility*. New York: Thomas Y. Crowell and Yale Plan Clinic. (P. 50.)

McCord, W. and McCord, J. (1960). *Origins of Alcoholism*. Stanford: Stanford University Press. (P. 67.)

Menninger, K. (1938). *Man Against Himself*. New York: Harcourt, Brace. (P. 164.)

Minister of Transport, reported in *The Times*, 12 December 1968.

Ministry of Health *Memorandum*, 1962. (P. 175.)

Moss, M. C. and Beresford Davies, E. (1968). 'A Survey of Alcoholism in an English County'. Privately printed, Geigy (U.K.) Ltd. (P. 20.)

Mouchot, G. (1955). 'Letter from France'. *International Journal on Alcohol and Alcoholism*, *1*, 75. (P. 73.)

Myers, E. (1954). 'Alcoholics and their familes'. *Case Conference*, *1*, 4 (P. 117).

Nolan, J. P. (1965). 'Alcohol as a factor in the illness of University Service patients'. *American Journal of Medical Science*, 249, 135. (P. 174.)

Nørvig, J. and Nielsen, B. (1956). 'A follow-up study of 221 alcohol addicts in Denmark'. *Quarterly Journal of Studies on Alcohol*, *17*, 633. (P. 164.)

Nylander, I. (1960). 'The children of alcoholic fathers'. *Acta Paediatrica Scandinavica*, 49, Supplement 121. (Pp. 71, 118.)

Parr, D. (1957). 'Alcoholism in general practice.' *British Journal of Addiction*, *54*, 25. (Pp. 19, 175).

Pittman, D. J. and Gordon, C. W. (1958). 'Criminal Career of the Chronic Police Case Inebriate'. *Quarterly Journal of Studies on Alcohol*, *19*, 11. (P. 164.)

Preston, B. (1958). *New Scientist*, 4, 1543. (P. 167.)

Rathod, N. H., Gregory, E., Blows, D. and Thomas, G. H. (1966) 'A two year follow-up study of alcoholic patients'. *British Journal of Psychiatry*, *112*, 683. (P. 148.)

Registrar General (1957). *Decennial Supplement, England and Wales, 1951. Occupational Mortality, Part 2, Vol. 2*. London: H.M.S.O. (P. 20.)

Registrar General (1962). *Statistical Review of England and Wales for the year 1959. Supplement on Mental Health*. London: H.M.S.O. (P. 19.)

Robins, E., Murphy, G. E., Wilkinson, R. H., Gassner, S. and Kayes, J. (1959). 'Some clinical considerations on the prevention of suicide.' *American Journal of Public Health*, 49, 888. (P. 165.)

Robins, L. N., Bates, W. M. and O'Neal, P. (1962). 'Adult Drinking Problems of Former Problem Children'. In *Society, Culture and Drinking Patterns*, ed. Pittman, D. J. and Snyder, C. R. New York: John Wiley & Sons. (P. 68.)

Robinson, M. W. and Voegtlin, W. L. (1952). 'Investigations of an allergic factor in alcohol addiction'. *Quarterly Journal of Studies on Alcohol*, *13*, 196. (P. 69.)

Schmidt, W., Smart, R. G. and Popham, R. E. (1963). 'The role of alcoholism in motor vehicle accidents'. In *Alcohol and Road Traffic*, ed. Havard, J. D. J. London: British Medical Association. (P. 167.)

Seebohm Rowntree, B. and Lavers, G. R. (1951). *English Life and Leisure*. London: Longmans. (Pp. 48, 49.)

Selzer, M. L. and Holloway, W. H. (1957). 'A follow-up of alcoholics committed to a state hospital'. *Quarterly Journal of Studies on Alcohol*, *18*, 98. (P. 147.)

Silkworth, W. D. (1937). 'Alcoholism as a manifestation of allergy'. *Medical Record*, *145*, 249. (P. 140.)

Skolnick, J. H. (1957). *The Stumbling Block*. Doctoral Dissertation, Yale University. (P. 52.)

Skutin, A. (1959). 'Sweden, Sequel'. In *Drinking and Intoxication*, ed. McCarthy, R. G. New Haven: College and University Press. (P. 169.)

Straus, R. and Bacon, S. D. (1951). 'Alcoholism and social stability'. *Quarterly Journal of Studies on Alcohol*, *12*, 231. (P. 129.)

Straus, R. and Bacon, S. D. (1953). *Drinking in College*. New Haven: Yale University Press. (P. 51.)

The Times, 30 April 1964. (P. 73.)

Trevelyan, G. M. (1944). *English Social History*. London: Longmans. (Pp. 53, 54.)

Ullman, A. D. (1962). 'First drinking experience as related to age and sex'. In *Society, Culture and Drinking Patterns*, ed. Pittman, D. J. and Snyder, C. R. New York: John Wiley & Sons. (P. 43.)

Wallerstein, R. S. (1957). *Hospital Treatment of Alcoholism*. London: Imago Publishing Co. Ltd. (P. 149.)

Wallinga, J. V. (1949). 'Attempted suicide: a ten year survey'. *Diseases of the Nervous System*, *10*, 15. (P. 165.)

Walton, H. J. (1961). 'Group methods in the psychiatric treatment of alcoholism'. *American Journal of Psychiatry*, *118*, 410. (P. 135.)

Walton, H. J., Ritson, E. B. and Kennedy, R. I. (1966). 'Response of alcoholics to clinic treatment'. *British Medical Journal*, ii, 1171.

Wolff, S. and Holland, L. (1964). 'A questionnaire follow-up of alcoholic patients'. *Quarterly Journal of Studies on Alcohol*, *25*, 108. (P. 149.)

Woodside, M. (1961). 'Women drinkers admitted to Holloway Prison'. *British Journal of Criminology*, January, 221. (P. 163.)

World Health Organization. Expert Committee on Mental Health (1952). *Alcohol Subcommittee Second Report*. W.H.O. Technical Report Series, No. 48. (P. 18.)

INDEX OF AUTHORS

SUBJECT INDEX